more than a walk

The Journal of a 16-Year-Old
*Hiker on the **Appalachian Trail***

Timothy F. Corey

7C's Marketing | San Antonio

Copyright © 2022 Timothy F Corey.

All rights reserved. No part of this publication may be reproduced, distributed, or transmitted in any form or by any means, including photocopying, recording, or other electronic or mechanical methods, without the prior written permission of the publisher, except in the case of brief quotations embodied in critical reviews and certain other noncommercial uses permitted by copyright law. For permission requests, write to the publisher, addressed "Attention: Permissions Coordinator," at the address below.

ISBN: 979-8-9864603-0-7 (Paperback)
ISBN: 979-8-9864603-1-4 (Hardcover)
ISBN: 979-8-9864603-2-1 (EBook)

Front cover design by: Peter Corey

Produced in association with 7C's Marketing, in the United States of America.

First printing edition 2022.

7C's Marketing
2186 Jackson Keller Rd
San Antonio, TX 78260

www.timhikes.com
www.7csmarketing.com

Dedicated to:

Aeriel Corey, my sister, without whom this adventure would never have happened.

Contents

Forward   1

Introduction   4

   1. It Begins   7

   2. New Hampshire Pains   20

   3. The Presidentials   37

   4. Maine   56

   5. The 100 Mile Wilderness   82

   6. Intermission   102

   7. A New SOBO start   107

   8. Enter Cameron   140

   9. Waynesboro   166

   10. Virginia Blues   175

   11. A 50 Mile Day   210

   12. Goodbye Virginia, Hello Tennessee!   218

   13. Smokies, Here We Come!   241

   14. The End Days   256

Forward

By Aeriel Corey

When I announced to my friends and family that I was going to hike the Appalachian Trail after I graduated from college, I was shocked and amazed that there wasn't a whole lot of interest in joining me. Who wouldn't want to quit their comfortable 1st world life for 5 months and live out of a 40-pound backpack, sleep on the ground, and walk 15-20 miles up and down mountains every day carrying said pack? What absurdity this world contains.

Only one person responded with the enthusiasm I had hoped for, and that was my 16-year-old brother Tim. Fortunately for both of us, my parents' desire to keep their teenage son in high school was surpassed by the fear of their daughter getting "raped, murdered, or eaten by wild animals alone" so, they agreed that he could skip school and go. This decision thrilled both of us, obviously.

Tim and I had always been good adventure buddies. The first day I had my driver's license and the freedom it entailed, I grabbed 10-year-old Tim and we drove to a San Antonio park we had visited many times with the family. We spent the day exploring all the brushy, dark, sketchy deer trails we had never been allowed to go on. We got lost, found hobo camps, got unlost, and eventually made it home scratched up, bruised, and grinning ear to ear. It was all downhill from there.

Tim's AT journal is as humorous as you may imagine a 16-year-old boy's take of walking from Maine to Georgia would be, and far more insightful. I was fascinated to read it and see how different his experience was from mine, despite walking all the same miles and sharing the same camps every night. His journal also happens to be free from persistent rumination about boyfriend problems, something I can't say about my own.

Today Tim lives a life that I admire and am secretly jealous of. While I am a corporate slave following a cookie-cutter career path and locked in golden handcuffs, he owns his own business, works at a bar, and is always 3 steps ahead of everyone else, thinking of the next business he will start or the next thing he can brew or create. He seems to be genuinely unaffected by anyone else's idea of what he should do with his life. He hiked the Pacific Crest Trail last year with his amazing girlfriend Megan and is already making plans to finish the Vermont Long Trail and the Continental Divide Trail in the near future. He is not discouraged for long by any kind of failure, seemingly just absorbing negative events and turning them into the next best thing. I like to think his unique and fearless approach to life started on the Appalachian Trail and I am so honored to have been a part of that adventure.

This is Tim's first book, but I am sure it won't be his last. Will it be a success? Who knows. The best part is, I don't think Tim particularly cares. When I was considering investing some of my dirty oil money in his first company he told me "You know what? Thanks, but probably don't invest in this one, it may not be super profitable. Invest in my 3rd or 4th company." He said this with no self-deprecation and with a smile on his face. I think that pretty much sums up what makes Tim great. Tim does Tim and doesn't care about the outcome. He knows that life consists of ups and downs, and that persistence with a smile will always pay off eventually: just like the Appalachian Trail.

Introduction

-

More Than A Walk is a journal written during my time on the Appalachian Trail. Within its pages lay my thoughts, feelings, struggles, and growth. I was 16, and my life was about to change forever...

I don't really remember how it happened. I don't know if it was a phone call, me hearing my sister talk about it and insisting I come along, or if she asked me to be polite while fully expecting our parents to say no. However it happened, and for whatever reason, I made a commitment to join my sister on a trip she was planning for the summer of 2014. In making this commitment I had unknowingly taken the first steps of an experience that would change me forever: Hiking the Appalachian Trail.

I was 16 years old, and like many 16-year-old boys in their sophomore year of high-school, my life was in turmoil for no particular reason. My growing desire for mental and physical independence from my parents, and the fading confusion of the hormone infested years of my early teenage life, often manifested itself in unhealthy ways. Girls, rebellion, sneaking out, work, questioning religion, football, school, and maturity; I was struggling to decipher what it meant to be a man and what it meant to be responsible for myself. At that time, the idea of escaping my home was an intoxicating one. Intoxicating, not because my home was bad (I had an incredibly wonderful and loving childhood), but because something inside me would explode if I didn't.

My sister would soon be graduating from Texas A&M University and her plan was to start out on the Appalachian Trail (AT) in May. Together, we capitalized on my parents' fear of her hiking alone and we were able to convince them to allow me to go along. As most of my peers would begin their summer binge of the latest video games, I would be embarking on a real-life journey to discover America and myself.

More Than a Walk is my journal written during my time spent on the Appalachian Trail. I have often revisited my journal since it was written, re-living memories, experiences, and lessons from that time.

I originally published this journal on my website *Timhikes.com* in 2021. I chose this date because I was about to leave for another adventure on the Pacific Crest Trail and I felt that it was finally time for me to share my experiences on the AT with those who were interested.

Within these pages you can follow along with my experiences all those years ago as I lived them. The good days, the bad, the happiness and the sadness, my emotions, thoughts, and feelings: the Appalachian Trail from the perspective of a 16-year-old stepping out for the first time into the world.

Note: When typing up this journal for print I had to make many corrections to my original usage of grammar and spelling. While reading, you will find apparent inconsistencies in the usage of tense. At times I speak in past tense, and at other times I speak in the present. These inconsistencies have been intentionally left and should serve as an indication of where I was when I made any particular entry.

Part 1

It Begins

Monday, May 12th
2014

Pre-hike Thoughts
-

My room seems smaller than normal, the walls feel like they are closing around me. I've never been claustrophobic, but today I understand how it must feel…. I need to get outside.

I must admit, I'm jealous. Aeriel (my sister) and my father are leaving tomorrow for the Appalachian Trail… and I'm stuck at home for another month to finish up my sophomore year of high school. It sucks. They are starting their trek at a place called the Delaware Water Gap (mile 1296.0 going North Bound) and hiking north to Maine from there. The plan, from what I understand, is to hike all the way north to Maine and then to get a ride back down to the Delaware Water Gap where we will hike south to Springer Mountain in Georgia. Aeriel informs me that this is called a "Flip Flop" and is in no way any less of an accomplishment than a normal North Bound Thru-Hike.

Of course, since I won't be joining them right away, there will be a large portion of the trail that I will miss. I wish I could just get out of here already. I'm excited and nervous about the AT. It'll be an adventure for sure!

It's raining tonight, the thunder booms and the lightning produces bright streaks across the sky. I'm looking forward to these types of nights on the trail.

Even the rain won't be too bad, I think.

I'm hoping to find a peace in the wilderness, especially on nights like these.

Monday, June 9th
One Month Later
-

    I am sitting in the car right now, riding along in the beautiful Vermont countryside. The Pine trees tower over the smaller trees and lush underbrush below. I see Birch, Maple, Oak, and many others I don't know. In just a few days I will be traveling amongst them.

I am reading Nietzsche:

    "If you wish to strive for peace of soul and pleasure, then believe; if you wish to be a devotee of truth, then inquire."

    So what? I can't find peace of soul and pleasure through inquiry? Through logic I can only find truth and not happiness? Or is truth happiness?

    I have a love-hate relationship with Nietzsche and the things he wrote. His words are so often empty and longing for something more... human. To this day I am still unsure of what Nietzsche would say is truth or what is the purpose of life, or even if there is truth or purpose in his opinion.

    I'm not sure what the purpose of life is either. I don't know if there is free will. I don't know if there is a God. I do know, however, that if there are answers to be found out about the nature of the universe or my own mind, the wilderness may be the best place to find them...

Thurs, June 12th
Day 0

Gear Choices and Criticisms

I don't think dad believes I am going to make it very far on the trail. We are at the Cabin (our family has a rustic log cabin on 20 acres of Vermont woods), just a few miles from where we are going to be picking up the Appalachian Trail, and he is heavily criticizing my gear choices.

After some research, I decided on wearing Trail Running Shoes instead of boots and I chose to bring a hammock and tarp instead of a tent. Lighter gear made sense to me, and my experience on the east coast suggests to me that I will never be too far away from a workable pair of trees. He is old school though, and I think the thought of hiking in anything besides the most tough and the most waterproofest of boots gives him anxiety. I promised mom that I would do my best not to butt heads with him too much. We will see how that goes…

Tomorrow we are leaving for the AT. I'm Excited and very nervous! Dad and Aeriel made it just over 300 miles in the last month through New Jersey, New York, Connecticut, Massachusetts, and the beginning portion of

Vermont. Dad and Aeriel have already hiked over 300 miles… and I am about to take my first ever steps with a backpacking backpack on. On top of that, Aeriel says that Vermont and New Hampshire are the hardest states on the trail… joy.

It's Rainy, has been for the last few days, and the downpour is supposed to continue well into the weekend. Naturally, dad is critiquing my shoes' lack of waterproofing, but my spirits aren't dampened!

I figure that even the best boots will likely be soaked through after a few days of rain, and my more breathable shoes will likely dry much faster. On top of that, if it's a hot day my feet will be thankful for the additional airflow. We shall see.

Friday, June 13th
Day 1

Two Tomatoes and a Green Bean
-

1st Day of the AT!!! It's somehow even more beautiful than I imagined it would be! The woods of Vermont are awesome like that. We started hiking north today where the Appalachian Trail crosses Route 4 (mile 1704.0) and have been tromping through rain and mud all day. A LOT of rain and mud. Mom dropped us off and commented on the fact that in our rain ponchos we looked like two tomatoes and a green bean!

Dad doesn't like the rain at all that much, but I don't mind it! I like how it makes the forest look misty and forgotten, much like how I imagine an old revolutionary battleground must have looked.

The fog rolls across the hills in front of me impeding my view… or maybe it is just the condensation on my glasses… damn glasses. They don't help too much when it's raining and just seem to serve as a collection point for copious amounts of water droplets.

We are at Stony Brook Shelter tonight, a short walk off the AT. We met some cool people here! Overall, we hiked about 10 miles, through the Vermont mountains, in the rain and mud! I'm tired, and my body already aches with pains I never knew a person could have. It was a great day!

Saturday, June 14th
Day 2

Ass Chafes

We just stopped hiking, hopefully for the day. I'm VERY happy about that. Around noon I started to get some really bad chafing in the ass region, some of the worst chafing of my life; its most definitely NOT fun.

Despite the drawbacks, the day was awesome. It was raining and muddy up till around noon (which is probably what kickstarted the chafing). I fell and landed on my butt only once and am quite lucky I did not hurt myself. Stupid slippery rocks. We stopped at a place called "the lookout" to eat lunch. There was an amazing view overlooking the green mountains of the Vermont countryside! Moments like that are why I love this trail. I know I have only been out for two days, but it feels like it has been weeks.

But yes, I'm chafing very very badly, my butt feels like it's been bitten by hundreds of fire ants. I can barely walk. I made my discomfort clear to my companions and insisted that I could go no further for the day. Dad isn't too happy because he doesn't want to stop. Honestly though, I don't care what he thinks at this point, I am in too much pain.

We are on top of a beautiful mountain and the wind is blowing through the trees, it's amazing. I am sitting in my hammock and am rocking slightly back and forth, the rushing of the wind through thousands of leaves that make up the canopy above me is refreshing and invigorating. It is a voice of nature that speaks tales of exploration and the unknown.

Sun, June 15th
Day 3

Up and Down and Up and Down
-

Okay, so maybe 16 miles doesn't seem like much to you, but you are probably used to driving to a restaurant some evenings, or maybe driving back and forth to work every day. Nice roads, pavement and, oh yeah, you have a car.

Try walking 16 miles in Vermont forest, up and down Vermont Hills. Up and down and up and down and up and down over and over and over again, all the while suffering from a terrible ass chafe... and this activity is expected to be carried on day after day after day!

Today I was lagging behind both Aeriel and Dad, going pretty slow. I am still in quite a bit of pain and found it to be increasingly more intolerable as the day went on. I have begun hypothesizing about potential treatments for the chafing. The consensus is baby powder – I will be sure to pick some up at my first town stop.

I almost fell into a brook today, barely catching myself at the last moment, so that was wonderful...

Even with all of that though, we made 16 miles to the Happy Hills Shelter. It's an interesting place made of stone instead of logs. It has one smaller opening in the front of the structure instead of the normal large opening on the side like most of the other shelters we have seen. The one downside? The mosquitoes are terrible!!! So many of the little shits!! They buzz buzz buzz around non-stop, and they attack any bit of skin you leave exposed. They seem to be attracted to the dark dampness insides of the shelter… too bad!

There is a glorious privy here too, the nicest one I have seen yet! "Privy" is just another term for an outhouse and most we have come across are small, cramped, smelly, and infested with flies. This one, by contrast, is roomy, well-engineered, and new. Dad says that if it starts to rain he may decide to sleep there. It is that nice!

Dinner tonight is mac and cheese, I'm excited for that! I'm starting to get super hungry and can't seem to eat enough! I estimate that I am burning between 4,000 and 6,000 calories a day out here, and I seriously doubt I am eating that much. The hiker hunger is real.

Part 2

New Hampshire Pains

Mon, June 16th
Day 4

Trail Magic

People are amazing out here. So happy and gracious, I haven't met a mean one yet! It's really refreshing and really helps to "restore faith in humanity".

Today we hiked 6 miles into Hanover, my first town stop. Hanover also marks the end of the Vermont portion of the trail and the beginning of New Hampshire. New Hampshire is reported to be the toughest state on the entirety of the trail. Steep climbs and mountains exposed to the elements await us here.

As we walked out of Vermont, we discovered two "trail magic" boxes that someone had left along the side of the road for the Appalachian Trail hikers. Free snacks!! "Trail Magic" is a somewhat frequent occurrence that can take on many different forms. The people who set up the trail magic are referred to as "Trail Angels". The people who leave trail magic are truly the most amazing and wonderful people to have ever lived in this world! So, to all the wonderful Trail Angels out there: Thank You. Your generosity is well appreciated by us hungry hikers.

We spent some time in Hanover resupplying our food and eating lunch with Uncle Gary who drove over to meet us. Uncle Gary and his wife, my Aunt Sarah, live in New Hampshire and seem excited to have us hiking in their backyard! They plan to come out and meet us whenever possible! We ate at this restaurant called Molly's where I got a hamburger! I'm not sure if it was my insatiable hunger or not, but I am pretty sure that it was the best hamburger I have ever eaten. So cheesy and fatty and gooey and delicious. I wish I had 2 more! Throughout the entire town of Hanover, I only saw one pretty girl. I don't know if there aren't many pretty girls in Hanover, or if my sweaty nastiness drove them away! Most likely the latter.

Now I am sitting in my hammock surrounded by dead trees that could fall at any moment. Our campsite was chosen partially out of necessity, but we (especially dad) are quite worried about a tree falling on us in the night. I certainly hope that they don't, that would be a poor end to my newly commenced journey.

Tuesday, June 17th
Day 5

Trail Names
-

Today started off very poorly. I was tired, and I ended up forgetting my Paracord (simple cordage which was originally created for use in parachutes) at our camp. I had hung up our food bags the night before and was so anxious to eat breakfast in the morning that I forgot to pack it back up after retrieving the bags. They say that the trail provides, but it seems as if it takes just as well.

Hanging food bags at night is necessary to keep bears, mice, and other creatures from stealing and eating it. It is not uncommon for mice to chew through layers of tent, backpack, and stuff sack in order to retrieve a morsal of Poptart. Bears aren't usually a problem, but certainly can be if they are especially hungry or in an area where they have become used to humans and their food. Either way, its better to be safe!

The hike today was particularly tiring, but I did very well! I think my body is finally starting to get used to the unique requirements of backpacking. First, we hiked up Moose Mountain (mile 1761.0) which wasn't too hard and yielded some pretty views of the countryside. After Moose Mountain we hiked up a real steep one which practically killed me. It was especially disheartening when Aeriel told me that Smarts Mountain, which would be our last climb for the day, was twice as tall and just as steep…

We ate lunch about 10 miles in at the edge of a cliff called Holts Ledge. Again, the view was stunning. Looking over the expanse of land and mountains extending in every direction in front of you yields a feeling that can't quite be described. Distance takes on a new meaning in the wilderness.

After lunch we began our hike to the foot of Smart Mountain. I had to get water, so Paco and Goat Gurrl started up the 2000ft mountain without me. "Paco" is my father's trail name, and "Goat Gurrl" is my sister's. Trail names are a tradition on many hiking trails and are often given based on the stories or oddities of the individual hiker

My Sawyer Mini, our water filter of choice, is super annoying. It filters water at about the speed I think a snail might hike up the mountain (so not much faster than me). Filtering water is quite an annoying task but is a simple safety measure one can take to avoid picking up any unwanted parasites or diseases. I don't imagine that it is so necessary at beautiful mountain streams such as the ones we have passed, but at lower elevations or near cow fields it is basically required!

While I was struggling to get the Sawyer Mini to filter water at anything more than a snail's pace, and considering collecting water straight from the brook, I met two older guys going the same place for the night I was: *The Fire Wardens Cabin.* Noticing my struggles, the younger of the two suggested that I buy the Sawyer Squeeze, a slightly heavier but much less annoying version of the same filter. That sounded like a good idea to me.

The climb up was tiring, but I found a second tank of gas somewhere deep inside of me and managed to catch up to and beat both Paco and Goat-Gurrl to the top!! That felt quite nice. Once the summit was reached, we found the old cabin we had heard about. It seemed so dark and sad, the inside was illuminated by only two grimed up windows at its front, and it appeared as if it had been forgotten about by all except those few travelers who happened upon it. Because of the cabin's drab appearance, all three of us decided we would sleep in the fire watchers tower which stood about 60 or 80 feet above us.

This fire tower, which has been out of official use for years, is a steel structure with a rickety wooden hut at the very top. The stairs to the top are narrow and wind up and up to a small trap door that opens to the inside of the hut. Occasionally a stiff breeze comes and sways the tower back and forth. It seems like it will fall at any second. It is a nerve-wracking experience. Hopefully it won't choose this night to do so! We have a full 360-degree view from the windows (some of which are broken) and can see both the distances we have come and the distances we have yet to go. The view is wonderful.

Altogether we went 17 miles today, up and down the hardest mountains so far. I'm proud. The hardest hike and the best views I have yet to experience.

Wednesday, June 18th
Day 6

A Pulled Tendon
-

Today we were planning to go 21 miles, our longest day yet, but on the way down from an especially annoying climb (Mount Cube) the tendon in my left thigh got pulled. A tang of horrible pain shot up my leg. I'm not entirely sure what caused the issue, but I can now barely walk. Putting any weight at all on my leg makes the pain so much worse.

I hobbled down from Cube Mountain and convinced dad to stop at *Ore Hill Campsite* for the night, about 12 miles from where we started. After discussing our options, Paco, Goat-Gurrl and I decided it would be prudent to take today and tomorrow as rest days before attempting to hike Mount Moosilauke. Hopefully I'll be okay.

I understand that injuries happen, but it's really frustrating to slow down right as I start to feel like I'm getting used to the miles. Mount Moosilauke is apparently the highest and toughest mountain we will be hiking for some time, and Aeriel thinks that it would be best to take it easy rather than to push on only to injure myself even more.

As usual, her logic is impeccable but does little to lessen the frustration.

Now we are sitting in our camp. Paco, Goat Gurrl, and the two guys we met yesterday are all enjoying the camping chair I brought! I'm not sure what inspired me to bring a chair on a backpacking trip, but I am certainly glad I did. It weighs about a pound and a half, or so, but the ability to sit comfortably anywhere provides me with immeasurable satisfaction. No hard rocks or dirty and muddy ground for me! My chair even inspired my trail name: Lay-Z-Boy! Not sure how I feel about that one, but I'm rolling with it! Aeriel also says that she is glad I brought it.

I am starting to view the woods like my home now. I went out to pee earlier and the forest just felt familiar, like I was supposed to be there. Something in the wilderness around me accepted my presence, I'm not sure exactly how to explain the feeling, but it was good.

Thursday, June 19th
Day 7

Moosilauke
-

Wow, it's the one-week mark for me on the trail! One full week in the woods without technology, showers, or flushing toilets! I am honestly not so surprised that I don't miss those things a whole lot. It feels like I've done and experienced so much in that time, it's crazy to think that I am only just starting. I can't wait to see what else this beautiful trail has in store for me.

Today we hiked 15.5 miles and up a 4000-foot incline to the top of Mount Moosilauke. The name Moosilauke translates to "Bald Place." The Native Americans who lived in the region called it this because the elevation was so high that the summit was well above the tree line. I think the mountain needs to be renamed to Mount Mussolini due to its infinite and very painful assent. The uphill battle just kept going and going and going and never ended. At least that's how it seemed.

4,000 feet of elevation gain… that's almost a mile of straight up into the sky. That's 8 Enchanted Rocks (a fun hike for anyone who happens to find themselves in the

Texas Hill Country) stacked up on top of each other!! Dad says that today is probably the hardest climb we will do the entire trip... I'm not so sure... something tells me that he may be wrong about that. We will see, I guess. My leg was feeling much better today, I tried to take it easy because I could feel that it was right on the edge of getting much worse. Hopefully it will only continue to heal.

We hiked to the top of Moosilauke and the pain and suffering of the climb gave way to an awe-inspiring 360-degree view of what looked like the entire world. We could see the White Mountains of New Hampshire in front of us, and the Green and Adirondack Mountains behind us. The true expanse of the world was stunning from that majestic spot. I didn't want to leave it, but once we got above treeline the wind got bad, really bad. Dad took a video with his phone, and despite him yelling, you could only hear the howling of the wind!

The temperature was dropping so, in the name of not freezing to death, we continued down the trail to our stop for the night: *Beaver Brook Shelter.*

Beaver Brook Shelter is the coolest shelter yet (in both temperature and awesomeness). It is basically located on the side of the mountain and has a great northern view framed by tall pines and a stary sky. We can see both the

Lafayette Mountain range and Mt. Washington in the distance. Mount Lafayette looks imposing, almost scary, like something out of an adventure book. The thought of having to climb it both frightens and excites me.

Friday, June 20th
Day 8

Realities Rushing Back
-

    Today started off well enough. My leg was feeling much better and we descended Mount Moosilauke along Beaver Creek. The trail was really steep and very slippery. There were portions of the walk where someone had attached re-bar loops into the rock face to act as a sort of ladder to assist hikers along the almost vertical "trail". Beaver Creek should probably be renamed beaver waterfall. For almost the entire decent we watched as it tumbled and fell through the terrain. It pooled in some areas, and in others it cascaded vertically right alongside us. It was picturesque. It was true beauty that only nature can provide.

    After our decent, in true Appalachian Trail fashion, we went right back up again toward Kinsman Ridge. I was feeling amazing, I was elated from the remarkable beauty all around me. I jumped ahead full of happy energy. Somewhere along the way, though, I pulled the stupid tendon in my leg again and the reality of life came rushing back. For the next 5 miles up Kinsman Mountain I was in excruciating pain once again. That wasn't fun at all. The huge variety of emotions that I feel out here, and the sheer extremes and intervals at which they emerge is shocking. In one moment, I am on top of the world, and in the next I am in the worst type of despair. Is this our natural state?

I am lucky that I can still walk at all. I will probably need to take it easy again for the next few days. I hope it gets better quickly; I really do.

Despite my leg, we eventually made it to Kinsman Pond Shelter. Some of the shelters in New Hampshire are apparently run by caretakers, people whose job it is to perform upkeep on nearby trails, to maintain the privy, and to collect $8 fees from each backpacker who finds his way there. Kinsman Pond is a beautiful place and the shelter and nearby camping sites are of the highest quality. So at least I can see where our fee is going. I volunteered to go pay the caretaker as an excuse to explore the area a bit more on my own. Total, we went 13 miles today!

Saturday, June 21st
Day 9

Retired Millionaire Banker
-

Today was a shorter day which, given the state of my leg injury, was fine by me. I slept wonderfully in the cool air of the New Hampshire alpine, and it was feeling much better by the time I woke up in the morning. It is amazing what a night of rest and sleep can do. Even so, our plan to take it easy for the day relieves my worry and nervousness. We are running low on food and have plans to stop in Lincoln to re-supply. It should be an easy downhill walk in.

About halfway to the road into Lincoln we stopped at a place called *Lonesome Lake Hut* to ask questions. Apparently, an organization called the Appalachian Mountain Club maintains the trails throughout a large portion of New Hampshire and have set up a network of expensive lodges, called *Huts*, throughout the region. These Huts, at about $125 per person per night cater to the high-end adventurers who want to experience the white mountains in relative luxury. We also learned that many of these huts allow thru-hikers to stay and eat leftovers for free in return for labor. These arrangements are called "work for stays". This sounds like a great deal to me!

It was at this Hut where we met Spock, a retired banker from Pennsylvania who saw no problem with forking out $125 a night for a bunk and a homemade meal! He was a really cool guy! Once we got to the road into Lincoln, we met up with Uncle Gary and Aunt Sarah who gave all of us (including Spock) a ride into town to resupply. Uncle Gary and Aunt Sarah brought us sandwiches which hit the spot quite nicely!

We spent a bit of time with Spock, who we hit it off with. He gave us his phone number and told us to call him if we were ever near the Delaware Water Gap and needed anything! Perhaps we will meet up with him again when we flip back down to the south.

We stopped for the night at a tent site halfway up Mount Lafayette or, what I have decided to call, "THE FORBIDDEN MOUNTAIN" due to its foreboding and menacing nature. Our campsite for the night is called *Liberty Springs Campsite*. The hike up was difficult and very steep, but also exciting. The idea of climbing such an imposing mountain made the effort worth-while. There are a lot of cool people to talk to and meet at this campsite. I love the trail for this reason; I've met so many interesting people from so many different walks of life. There aren't many places in the world where retired millionaire bankers, high-school students, professional engineers, and recent college graduates all come together to fight for a common goal. This trail is truly unique and amazing.

Part 3

The Presidentials

Sunday, June 22nd
Day 10

"The Forbidden Mountain"

It seems like the harder the hiking is, the more beautiful the views and scenery. Today was certainly no exception to this rule. We started off with summiting Lafayette Mountain via Little Haystack Mountain, Lincoln Mountain, and Franconia Ridge. I had given this mountain the nickname "The Forbidden Mountain" due to its imposing nature from miles away. The reality of the experience, however, was quite exceptional.

The entire ridgeline was well above tree line and seemed treacherous. Portions were rocky and steep. The constant 360-degree views, however, were beyond description. There were quite a few other people out hiking the ridge as well, even a few families with younger children. It was a unique and beautiful thing experiencing such beauty with other people. Everyone I passed seemed to be as engaged and as espoused with the mountain as I. We smiled at each other as we passed, exchanged pleasantries, and even got to know each other a bit as we leapfrogged back and forth. Despite knowing nothing about these people, it was as if we were connected through shared experience and sheer humanity. Again, it was beyond words.

Lafayette Mountain gave way to Mt. Garfield, and Mt. Garfield gave way to South Twin Mountain, both tough and beautiful climbs in their own right. We passed a few more Huts and even stopped inside one for some baked goods. Eventually we came across this amazing hill that looked like what I imagine the hills of Ireland must look like. Infinite shades of green: the grass, the trees, the bushes, rolled their way into a grey and overcast sky. The smell of the air was pure and fresh.

There is this magnificent bird that is common on these mountains that I like quite a bit. It has a black color on top that fades into a white/grey on its bottom. It seems to happily flutter from bush to bush looking for seeds or insects. I imagine myself as this bird, skipping along in this infinite beauty, worried only about where my next meal is coming from. It seems a pure existence.

Dad didn't do too well today. I think the miles may have been a bit too much… We are staying at Guyot Shelter, yet he is sleeping on a tent pad in his sleeping bag without his tent. He even denied Goat-Gurrl's and my request to set it up for him. I hope it doesn't get too cold.

He has been out here for quite some time now (300 miles longer than me, remember), and I can tell that he misses my mom. The mountains have been tough lately, but maybe things will get better in Maine!

Monday, June 23rd
Day 11

The Appalachian River
-

Today we started the Presidential Ridge, about 23 miles of above tree-line ridge walking over some of the tallest and most imposing mountains in New Hampshire: Mount Webster and Mount Jackson, Mount Pierce and Mount Eisenhower, Mount Franklin and Mount Monroe, all building up to the tallest point in New England and the second tallest on all of the Appalachian Trail: Mount Washington.

The first 8 miles after leaving camp where an easy flat and downhill that partially went through this cool alpine swamp area that looked like the perfect habitat for bears. I didn't see any, but I am sure they were there! After the flats we started a nice (and by nice, I mean death-like) uphill to Webster Mountain.

The weather at this point turned quite ugly for us. The wonderful sun of yesterday faded away behind a thick layer of grey-black clouds and the fog, which seemed to rush in all at once from nowhere, was accompanied by the occasional spout of heavy rain. Some parts of the trail where so worn down from use that the rain found it to be the easiest spot to collect in and rush down the mountain. This had the effect of basically turning the trail into a waterway. Dad referred to it as "The Appalachian River." My shoes never stood a chance! They won't be dry for quite some time I imagine.

From Webster we did Jackson, then after 18 miles from the start we ended at Mizpah Hut and Camp, our stop for the evening.

A girl at the hut informed us the caretaker at the campsite, Dave, was really cool. All the girls at the Hut were quick to confirm. It was clear that they had quite the crush. We made our way down a side trail to the campsite and met the illustrious Dave and, believe it or not, he was pretty cool. He had a ukulele and played it quite well. Aeriel got to talking to him and agreed to deliver a letter for him to a friend of his who is a caretaker at a future location. A cool side quest if you ask me!

Tuesday, June 24th
Day 12

Mount Washington
-

Today was spent entirely along the Presidential Ridge. The bad weather of yesterday continued today and never cleared. The fog constantly interchanged between a slight overshadow to a full on thick-as-pea-soup envelopment. There were moments we couldn't see much further than 10 or so feet in front of us. This made it difficult finding our way from cairn (the rock piles that marked the trail) to cairn.

The rain was also intense. There were moments it was coming down so hard that it felt like I was being knocked on the head by BBs. It wasn't just falling from above either. The wind was blowing so hard that, at times, it came at us horizontally. Sadly, all the fog and rain kept us from seeing any views on what was supposed to be one of the most awesome portions of the trail. There was one moment, though, where I was sitting on a rock watching the fog run past the mountainside. It flowed along like a river of smoke, being pushed by gale force winds up the mountain. It was grand. I like fog.

Around noontime we summited Mount Washington. On our way up to the top there were wind gusts that practically blew us off our feet. Our baggy rain ponchos certainly didn't help matters - they acted like parachutes every time we tried jumping from one boulder to the next. There were moments where dad said he purposefully jumped further to the right of where he intended to land because he knew the winds would carry him to where he needed to be. He was not exaggerating.

I have heard stories of people dying on these mountains, and I can easily see how. I am glad that I am not hiking alone. One could easily lose their footing on these boulders and break a leg, or worse. In these poor conditions it could be days before someone stumbles by. A death sentence, I would imagine.

Aeriel and I summited Mount Washington and started down the other side when Dad yelled at us and asked if we were going inside with him. Inside?!?! What?!? Apparently, there is a visitor center, restaurant, and weather museum on top of Mount Washington that Aeriel and I walked right past and missed because of the incredibly thick fog. The only reason we didn't pass it up never to return is because Dad already knew it was there.

Despite the weather, there were a bunch of people inside many of whom were fat and out of shape. Apparently, there is a train and a road to the top and physical activity is not a prerequisite for purchasing a ticket. It was very weird seeing these people on top of a mountain that we just struggled for days through the worst possible conditions to get to... it was almost unfair. It just goes to show the level at which humanity has conquered nature and have bended it to our will. We learned from weather reports that for the last couple of days we have been hiking through visibility reaching as little as 10 feet and gusts of wind that reached up to 70 MPH.... as fast as a category 1 hurricane. We spent some time in the visitor center enjoying the reprieve from the weather. We ate hotdogs and watched the masses of tourists come and go.

We barely made it to Madison Spring Hut before sunset. Dad was getting worried and stressed about making it in time. I understand his sentiment, I didn't want to get caught out above tree line in such bad weather either, but his stress/panic certainly wasn't helping. We ended up doing a "work for stay" at Madison Hut. The people were really nice and it was good to do some real work other than walking. We scrubbed ovens and cleaned floors. The "leftovers" we received after the paying guests had eaten were glorious.

After food and work I talked to this cute botanist working in the mountains. She is a caretaker of a campsite in Maine, and she told us not to forget to come by and say hi to her once we got there! Just another side quest on this glorious adventure.

Wednesday, June 25th
Day 13

The Worst Day of Dad's Life
-

We went a total of 14 miles today through continuous rain and fog. We hiked down and out of the Presidentials, past Pickham Notch, then directly back up into the Wildcat Mountains. Yes, there is more than one Wildcat Mountain, there is a Wildcat Mountain Peak A, a Wildcat Mountain Peak B, all the way to Wildcat Mountain peak E. The Appalachian trail goes over E, D, C and A. Of course, the rain and fog never stopped. We were facing torrential conditions and a "trail" that was constantly about a foot deep in freezing cold rushing water. We saw Spock again as well and hiked with him for a bit!

The going was steep, rocky, and slippery, and Dad was not having it. I don't blame him for not enjoying it, I don't blame him for worrying that we wouldn't make it to our camp in time, I do blame him, however, for taking what was a sub-optimal situation and making it worse by trying to force march Aeriel and me through it all with no breaks. There was a moment where Aeriel stopped to get a pack of raisins out of her pack because she was hungry, and dad freaked out over her delaying our entry to camp. Sure, the trail was wet, steep, and dangerous, but it is made more dangerous by not having any breaks and not being able to keep your energy up with food. My brother says that backpacking is like riding a motorcycle: you have to go your own pace, or it can become dangerous.

Dad told us a story about a time when he and my mother were hiking on the Long Trail in Vermont in similar circumstances. They got caught out in the dark, in the rain and cold, and almost missed their shelter. They almost passed by in the dark and only found it when, quite fortuitously, someone inside opened the door and flashed a light. A scary situation for sure. The wilderness can be a dangerous and unforgiving place.

We did make it to Cater Notch Hut before sundown, no problems. Perhaps the forced march was worth the effort despite its misery. Maybe it saved us from a cold and wet night without a shelter. Maybe it saved us from hypothermia. We will never know. Overall, it was a tough day that tested our will, our minds, and our perseverance. Dad says it was the worst day of his life…

Thursday, June 26th
Day 14

A Day of Mental Recovery
-

Today was good, the weather began to clear up, and the walking was mostly downhill and quite enjoyable. It was almost a shock when the sun shone brightly enough for us to see our shadows! I had forgotten that I had one of those. We did have a few mountains to climb, but nothing like the terrain we have been struggling through in the last few days. We even got to see a few views! Shocker, I know.

For almost the whole day we were hiking out of the mountains down toward our next re-supply location: Gorham, New Hampshire. After the last few days, I'm excited to spend a bit of time in town. It will feel good to see civilization again! We stopped for lunch at Imp Campsite where Aeriel delivered the note Dave had given her. Side quest complete.

We met three college graduates who looked as though they were having the time of their lives: The Professor, Thumper, and one other guy whose name I now forget. All three of them started at Katahdin and plan to SOBO Thru-Hike the trail. Maybe we will see them again when we flip back south! We discussed the upcoming trail for us, and it sounds easier than what we have come through. This matches what we have heard from other people and our research. I do believe the hardest part of our hike is complete!

Hopefully these three SOBOers will have better weather and an easier time than we did!

We are staying tonight at Rattle River Shelter, only a couple miles from the road to Gorham. So far, I have been out for two weeks and have come near 190 miles. That's 13 or 14 miles a day on average… amazing! At least I think so, especially considering that the portion of the trail I have completed is supposed to be the most difficult.

Tomorrow we will be in Gorham, and soon after that we will be in Maine!!

Friday, June 27th
Day 15

Among, but not a Part
-

Today was an amazing, wonderful, restful, and altogether delightful day in Gorham. We woke up this morning like regular, packed up, and had a wonderfully flat/slightly downhill walk to the road into Gorham. The forests were delightful, and the walking was easy. Even the birds sang out in joy for us filling the forest with chipper contentment. We got to Route 2 and were, once again, picked up by Aunt Sarah and Uncle Gary who shuttled us into the quaint little town of Gorham and to a waiting hotel with a shower.

Now, a shower might sound commonplace and ordinary for you. In fact, you probably use one almost every day. Not so for me… it seems like literal years since I last took a shower, and the dirt and grime that came off me and circled the drain only solidified that fact. I may have paused to be disgusted at myself if it hadn't felt so good. My shoes and clothes were so bad I decided to just walk into the shower with everything on. I peeled off my clothes and washed them at the same time as myself. What I thought was a tan line on my legs from my socks ended up just being an especially tough patch of dirt that disappeared with harder than normal scrubbing.

The hotel washcloth never stood a chance. By the time I was through, the once bright white and soft material was begrimed into such a pale-brownish state that I half considered throwing it out to save the cleaning lady from having to pick it up.

Dinner was as equally glorious as the shower; we went to an all-you-can-eat (AYCE) Chinese buffet called Dynasty Buffet where we had plate after plate of the most wonderful food we have ever eaten. I'm talking shrimp, egg rolls, crab, sushi, beef, chicken, pot stickers, ice cream, everything I had ever dreamed about and more. I tell you what, I can guarantee the restaurant lost out on that one…. Dad says he was disappointed because he couldn't physically eat as much as he wanted!!

It was strange being back in society again. There were a bunch of people all wearing bright orange shirts at the table next to us. How odd. There were tons of people, all living normal lives doing normal things. Then there is me. I felt as if I was an outcast returning home in secret: among, but not a part.

Saturday, June 28th
Day 16

Enter Gizmo

This morning we spent most of our time sleeping late and digesting our food from the night before. When we did finally leave the picturesque little mountain town that is Gorham, and when we did finally get dropped off back at the trail, and when we did finally wave Aunt Sarah and Uncle Gary goodbye, we turned our attention toward Mount Hayes, Cascade Mountain, and our goal for the night: Trident Col Campsite. Maine, here we come!

Most of the hike was uneventful, the weather was finally nice, and the trail wasn't too steep or deadly. I did, however, have some issues with my Achilles tendon that started to get super tight and hurt as we walked up our initial ascent. I walked backwards up the hill for a bit as an attempt to stretch it, but it didn't help too much. I'm not sure what the issue with it was, but after a few miles it loosened up and started to feel much better.

A bit past the summit of Mount Hayes I ran into an interesting character. He had a bushy black beard, wore a wrinkled and partially faded Indiana Jones Hat, carried a large pack, a thin wooden staff, and sported a utility belt with a large hunting knife, a hatchet, a very large can of bear spray, and a few other odds and ends attached to it...This had to be the fabled hiker Gizmo: a wild individual Aeriel had told me about who, having no experience, and having done zero research, set off from the tip of Florida for the Appalachian trail. That's right, he hiked over 800 miles through the heat and crocodile infested swamps of Florida before even stepping on the AT. And now he was in New Hampshire, within spitting distance of his end goal.

Gizmo got his name from those numerous odds and ends he had which, I am sure he never actually found a use for, but carried nonetheless. I asked him how much his pack weighed, and he said something along the lines of:

"I'm not too sure, probably never less than 50 pounds."

We got to talking about the trail and about Spock who apparently wasn't very far ahead. Aeriel was quite happy once she caught up to us. She had been hoping to see Gizmo again for quite some time! Gizmo carried on and promised to tell Spock hi for us if he saw him at the next campsite.

We made it to our campsite after a wonderful and relaxing day. It is good to be back on the trail again. The towns are nice, but I never feel as happy in them as I do in the woods.

Part 4

Maine

Sunday June 29th
Day 17

MUDs in Maine!
-

We did 14 miles today and crossed over into Maine, a huge landmark for me! Crossing from New Hampshire into Maine marked the completion of the first full state I have walked through on my Appalachian Trail journey.

So far, I have hiked 212 miles, 160 of which have been in the beautiful and rugged state of New Hampshire. At this point I feel as if I have been tried by fire (or in the case, by rain), and am well on my way to hiking the entirety of the AT.

Having never attempted it before, I have been thrown headfirst into the world of backpacking and have come out victorious! I have seen the lows, I have suffered injuries, I have met with difficulty and conditions I never expected, yet I am still walking on. The last mountain we summited in New Hampshire was Mount Success, a fitting end to the first stage of my journey.

The entire day so far has been ups and downs. Typical AT. All the "MUDs" got to dad; I think. The term "MUDs" stand for: Meaningless Ups and Downs... of which there are plenty to go around! All in all, it was a great day!

We ate lunch on top of Success Mountain and we passed quite a few SOBOS and one other person who had my same shoes! That's 3 people I have run into so far with the *La Sportiva Wildcats*.

We are spending the night at Full Goose Campsite with a guy named Coacu (what is that?) and two other kind of chunky guys. One of the chunky guys just let out a massive fart which I heard despite being quite a way away in my hammock. I don't know if he wanted it heard or not, but it basically shook the ground. It felt like an earthquake shook the trees my hammock is tied too. I'm in shock.

Anyway, I'm hoping it doesn't rain tonight. It's starting to look pretty iffy, and I don't feel like getting wet.

Monday, June 30th
Day 18

The "Disney Land" of the AT
-

I have said this before, and I am sure I will say it again, It's really cool all the people you meet and get to talking to out here. I think that it's my favorite part of this experience so far. There are so many different types of people from all walks of life. At the shelter tonight I met 3 guys doing a loop trail and a South-Bound hiker. I had a great time talking to them all. It is always fun discussing the trail with the SOBOs. Their experiences and stories of what lies ahead of us in Maine are exciting! I am sure they enjoy hearing about what lies in wait for them in NH as well.

They say that less than 1 in 5 people who set out on the trail reach their goal of finishing the entire thing. I wonder how many of these people I am meeting will make it? I wonder if I will. I am loving it so far and have no plan to stop!

This morning we started out by hiking down into the Mahoosuc Notch, a one-mile portion of the trail between Fulling Mill Mountain and Old Speck Mountain. This mile has the reputation of being "the hardest mile on the AT'. It certainly was. The Mahoosuc Notch isn't incredibly steep, but the network of huge boulders and deep crevices makes it almost impossible to navigate. Some of the crevices are so deep that snow lingers without melting year around.

We inched along crawling up rocks, taking off our packs, squeezing through small spaces, and jumping around from boulder to boulder. There were moments we had to climb hand over hand straight up!

There were a few mishaps (dad fell backwards onto his backpack), but overall, it went smoothly and was actually quite fun! One SOBO we passed referred to it as "The Disney World of the AT!". The idea being you just have to approach such obstacles with the proper mindset. It's much easier getting through a tough portion of trail if you look at it as a potentially fun activity instead of tedious and difficult work. Perhaps this is good advice for many things in life.

The 1 mile of the Mahoosuc Notch ended up taking us about 2 hours to complete. When it was all said and done, we totaled about 12 miles for the day and ended at Baldpate Lean-To, a shelter halfway up a pretty steep climb. I feel like I could have hiked more.

I believe I have thoroughly found my trail legs. The term "trail legs" is used to refer to a hiker's physical conditioning. When they have been found a backpacker has been through the worst of the physical pain, and their body is now used to the unique requirements and stresses of long-distance trips.

Tuesday, July 1st
Day 19

A Sad Goodbye
-

This morning was a beautiful one. On our way down from Baldpate Mountain, about a mile from a road that leads to Andover, we stopped at a wonderful mountain stream to gather water. It was beautiful day and the sunshine filtered down through the leaves and sparkled off the rushing water. Out of nowhere, though, Dad announced that he would be getting off the trail at the road and that he didn't plan on coming back.

This announcement took both me and Aeriel off guard. I wasn't sure what to say, and I am still not sure how I feel. I think the last few weeks have been pretty tough on him. He has made it clear that he really misses mom. I imagine that the rain and weather we have faced did not help things either.

So, as it was, we walked past Dunn Notch, collected Dad's spare snickers bars, and said our goodbyes at East B Hill Road into Andover. Dad was picked up by the owner of a nearby Hostel, and before we knew it, he was off the trail and heading home. All-in-all he hiked over 600 miles from the Delaware Water Gap to Andover Maine, through some of the toughest and most dangerous portions of the trail. It is an amazing feat for anyone, and a feat that I have nothing but respect for.

They say that one should never quit the trail on a bad day. I assume this rule is meant to keep you from making a rash decision that you will regret later. The trail has its fair share of very low lows, but it also has many incredible highs. It's easy to quit when you are feeling awful. If on a good day, however, you decide it may not be worth it any longer, maybe it makes sense to pull the plug. Dad didn't quit in the misery of a torrential downpour, he didn't quit during one of our many cold and dangerous ascents, he persevered though the toughest parts of the trail and, only after persevering through the worst and making it out to a better day, did he decide it was time to move on. It was a decision that I imagine was not made lightly.

After saying our sad goodbyes to dad, Aeriel and I hiked the gentle hills of Myman mountain and then hiked straight down into Sayer Notch and straight back up over 1500 feet of elevation in less than one mile to Moody Mountain. The steepness was staggering and incredibly tiring, but we made it through. Tonight, we are camping near South Arm Road. We hiked a total of about 18 miles: a good day for hiking, but a sad day nonetheless.

Wednesday, July 2nd
Day 20

No Rain, no Pain, no Maine!
-

Day 20, wow! It's crazy to think that I have been out here for almost 3 weeks. I also crossed my 250 mile mark today as well. So exciting!

We stared this morning by hiking up Old Blue Mountain. The scenery was amazing. The jagged rocks and protruding landscape of New Hampshire faded away and something different replaced it. There is moss everywhere, and the ancient forests of Maine seem ever wilder and more untouched. It is as if they have been here for thousands of years without being bothered. They probably have...

The White Mountains in New Hampshire are one of the most used portions of the AT and Maine, by contrast, is one of the most remote. You can really tell. For the most part, we will be hiking further away from towns and roads. The towns that we do come across will be smaller and more remote themselves. Fewer people, less disturbed woods, and wilder! I can't wait! It has been rainy and overcast today, but that doesn't change the beauty of the wilderness!

In fact, I think it complements and heightens it. No Rain, No Pain, No Maine!

We caught back up with Gizmo and Spock as well. It's good to see them again! Aeriel is happy about finding Gizmo. I do think she may have a crush. We stumbled upon him eating a strange mixture of things from a plus sized zip-lock bag. When we asked him about it, he informed us that to save money he buys large amounts of oatmeal, peanuts, raisins, and chocolate chips all at once and mixes them together as a sort of trail-mix to eat in the coming weeks. We decided to call this mixture "The Gizmo Mix". It is actually pretty good! Chocolate for the short energy boost, oats for the long burn, peanuts for protein, and raisins for everything else! Cheap, calorie dense, and tasty. Apparently when he has extra money, he replaces the chocolate chips with M&M's, and the regular peanuts with Honey Roasted ones.

We are at a shelter tonight called Sabbath Day Pond Lean-To. On the other side of the pond there is a dead moose. It is sad! The first moose I see, and its dead and decomposing. I suppose it is nature though, the way of the world, but it is still sad. I really want to see a live moose. It's on my AT bucket list for sure!

Thursday, July 3rd
Day 21

The Wings of Chance
-

Rangeley, a small town in Maine, is a wonderful place. What really makes it stand head and shoulders above the rest is: The Hiker Hut. The Hiker Hut is a glorious hostel run by a man named Steve and his wife. The Hiker Hut is located on a beautiful grassy clearing and is run completely off the grid. No running water, no electricity, nothing. There are two beautiful buildings on site, a bunkroom with a porch completed by an outdoor kitchen area, and a small A-Frame structure with a big sunflower painted on the roof. The owners are some of the nicest people I think I have ever met and make both breakfast and dinner for their guests over a large fire situated in the middle of the property. They also provide shuttles into and back from town for re-supplies.

The "bath" is located down a dirt trail and is a wonderful swimming hole that has been cleared out in the brook that runs through their property. I am happy to report that I took full advantage of this "bath" and skinny dipped for the first time in my life! It was exciting, but very chilly!

Steve told us about a lake in town that rented out paddle boards, so Aeriel and I went and took full advantage. There I was, laying down in the middle of the lake, starring straight up into to blue sky. There were a few very fluffy white clouds. It was strange knowing that I walked to this place, and that I would be walking again from it. Maybe never to return. It wasn't my home, and it wasn't a place that I would ever have come to in my normal life. I am just a passerby brought to it by the wings of chance, yet that made it all the more beautiful.

We decided to take advantage of being so close to a town and celebrated the Fourth of July a day early. Aeriel and Gizmo bought some beers in town, and we had a good night of celebrations by the campfire! Steve managed to make some of the best popcorn I have ever had in a big Dutch Oven pot over the fire. A wonderful evening with wonderful people!!

Aeriel and I both loved The Hiker Hut, and were talking about maybe taking a zero tomorrow, but we met this SOBO hiker who had been "trapped" for over a week. At first, he was just waiting for his mail to arrive, then he was waiting for the post office to open again, then he just didn't want to leave. He warned us of this place's unique tendency to trap you in. Not wanting to fall prey to the same trap (and because of our lack of money), we decided to take his advice and leave the next morning.

Friday, July 4th
Day 22

Gizmo Does, I Suppose
-

Fourth of July! Happy birthday America!! This morning we woke up to an amazing breakfast at the Hiker Hut. Steve, the amazing person that he is, warned us of incoming weather then bid us farewell. We were soon on our way.

The weather started off well enough, but Steve's warning soon became a reality as the wind picked up and grey clouds began to roll in from the distance. At this point in my journey I am quite used to rain so, because we weren't planning on hiking along many cliffs, I figured we would be alright. From Rangeley, Aeriel, Gizmo, and I continued north up Saddleback Mountain.

Though it was strange being with someone else all day long, spending time with Gizmo certainly had its moments. On the top of Saddleback Mountain he jumped up and, with his normal level of bravado, pulled out a pair of binoculars to look at the view. Who carries binoculars while backpacking?!? Gizmo does, I suppose. I asked if I could take a look and he happily obliged. I'm not sure if I did something wrong, if they were some special kind of binoculars, or what the deal was, but I couldn't see a thing out of them. Only what seemed to be layers of dust, dirt, and grime built up on the lenses. Not wanting to mention it, I handed them back and thanked him for letting me look. He put them back up to his eyes and went right back to surveying the landscape. A wonder if I ever saw one.

I was excited to make it to Poplar Ridge Lean-To, the shelter at which the cute botanist caretaker I met in the New Hampshire Whites worked at (refer to day 12). Sure enough, she was there! She was as cute as I remembered, so we talked for a bit. She, too, warned us about the incoming weather but, since it was still early, we decided to continue.

We finished our day at a gravel road we found. We were only a mile or so from a shelter, but we decided that the road would make for a nice, flat, and comfortable camping location. I was having some issues removing some stubborn underbrush to make room for my hammock, so Gizmo lent me his hatchet. Who carries a hatchet on a thru-hike?!?! Gizmo does, I suppose.

Saturday, July 5th
Day 23

Flooding Tents
-

    I was awoken from my slumber sometime early this morning by Aeriel. She informed me that her tent had flooded in the night and that she would wait for me at the upcoming shelter. Not fully understanding her words in my half-asleep state, I said "okay" and fell back to my warm and comfy hammock. It was only when I woke up a few hours later and found a puddle where Aeriel's tent once was that the gravity of her situation fully set in. Gizmo was there packing up his tent and told me that he got flooded as well but was able to stay mostly dry. Aeriel, it would appear, was not so lucky. I had no issues in my hammock and my tarp did wonders at keeping away the elements. I finished packing up my things and took off down the trail with Gizmo.

    I found Aeriel exactly where she promised: at the Spaulding Mountain Lean-to, the next shelter down the trail. She was sitting in the shelter, covered by a sleeping bag, shivering uncontrollably, and smoking a hand rolled cigarette that another hiker was kind enough to provide to her. She survived, but it didn't look like she was all that happy! Apparently, she had set up her tent in a divot on the side of the road, and as the rain fell it pooled at that exact spot. Not fun.

Once Aeriel warmed up a bit and started feeling better, we carried on up to Spaulding and Sugarloaf Mountains. We found a plaque commemorating the last section of the AT that was completed. Cool! The day was looking up when, at the bottom of a steep decline, we ran into the Carrabassett River.

This normally simple river crossing was flooded very badly and was raging at high speeds. It appears all the rain we received last night decided to rush down this particular river all at once. The wooden plank typically used to cross had been washed away, and the rocks that it normally sat upon where completely submerged.

Aeriel and I scouted for a bit up and down stream but couldn't find anywhere to cross that wouldn't pose substantial risk of falling. The water was simply too powerful. Around that time, Gizmo showed up and began scouting the same. After a while, he found a spot he decided he wanted to cross at. Being the first to admit to how dangerous the idea was, he stripped down to his underwear and crossed once without his pack to see if he could do it, back again, and once more with his pack carried above his head. Once on the other side he yelled a victorious yell, received cheers from those of us still on the other side, sat for a bit, and then continued down the trail and out of sight.

We spent the rest of the day on the riverbank waiting for it to settle down. A hiker girl named Milky, and a British Chap (whose name I forget), joined us and decided that they too would wait for the morning to cross. Milky informed everyone that the weather we experienced last night was from a very strong tropical storm that managed to blow its way this far north. We had no choice but to spend the night by the river, so I found a nice spot for my hammock and set up. Everyone else is having problems finding a flat spot big enough to set up their tents, just another win for the hammock!

I am set up in the prettiest spot yet. I have a perfect view both upstream and downstream along the river and of the sunset glistening off the raging waters. The sky is clearing up. I think the rain is done, so I'm hoping we will be able to continue tomorrow!

Sunday, July 6th
Day 24

The Awe of a Place
-

This morning the Carrabassett River was much less imposing. It seemed like its flow was about back to normal. We were able to find the wooden plank, replace it back to its spot, and cross without issue. To everyone's surprise we found Gizmo still on the other side just getting out of his abnormally large three-person tent (when asked about the excessively large tent, he told us that he bought it thinking the extra room would be nice though, if he had to re-do it, would get a two-person). Apparently, fording the river was all the excitement he needed for the day and decided to stop short of his 20-mile goal to wait for us.

We carried on north up the excessively steep Crocker Mountain. We, of course, have gotten quite used to 1,000-foot-every-mile climbs but this one was particularly bad! It seemed like for about half a mile we were walking straight up. My legs were not happy! We ate lunch at ME Route 27 and then got a hitch into Stratton to resupply. Afterward we started up Bigelow Mountain which is now my new favorite mountain range.

Walking up its ancient slopes was like entering a different world. A thousand different colors of green, moss-grown boulders the size of houses, and trees seemingly as old as time itself met us at every bend. The summit, which stood above the tree line, looked out over miles of wilderness. Dozens of alpine lakes with crystal clear water speckled the landscape before us. I considered for a second never returning to civilization. Maybe it was out, surrounded by all of this, where true purpose and happiness is to be found.

Struck by the sights and the experiences of the moment, we made camp in a small notch below two of the main peaks. We had already gone about 17 miles for the day and a night in this spot would be a night to remember.

As the fiery colors of sunlight faded into a twilight that overtook the alpine valleys, the wind picked up and we heard a yell. Not a normal yell, but one which comes from a deep place. It was a yell of triumph, of pride. The sound could have come from an animal, I wouldn't be surprised if it had, but a few minutes later, Gizmo materialized out of the woods and joined us in camp. Apparently, the awe of this place was shared among all who witnessed it.

Monday, July 7th
Day 25

A Different Kind of Animal
-

The pain and difficulty of Maine does not come from its mountains. At this point I have become quite accustomed to difficult climbs and the constant struggle of burning thighs; Maine is a different kind of animal. The highs and profound enlightenment of Bigelow Mountain faded as we walked away from it and, as with life, the trail often follows good with bad.

As we descended Bigelow, we didn't immediately start heading back up another mountain as we had come to expect. Instead, the terrain flattened out and the rocks gave way to water and mud. We were walking into the dark and mosquito infested swamps of Maine.

Luck was on our side; it was a beautiful sunny day. The few rays of sunshine that trickled down through the dense canopy of leaves were a wonderful reprieve from the soggy, grimy ground and treacherous roots which carpeted the forest floor. Portions of the trail were so overtaken by these tree-roots that we were walking atop of them with nothing but air and mud below. Deet became our new best friend, spreading it over every exposed portion of my skin made me feel as if I was giving myself cancer. It did little to deter the thousands of mosquitos dive-bombing me. They went for my eyelids, the back of my ears, my neck, everywhere. It was awful.

The day was long, the distance was tough, but I am tougher!! In total, the majority of our 25-mile day was spent fighting the mud, roots, and mosquitoes, but the lack of mountains helped us push all the way to the striking Pierce Pond. I am sitting in my hammock considering the wonders of my existence. It would be peaceful except for the dozens of French speaking Canadians who are sharing our campground. They are loud and quite insufferable. It appears as if the serenity of this place has been lost on them.

Tuesday, July 8th
Day 26

The Kennebec Ferry
-

One reason we hiked so far yesterday was to get as close as possible to the Kennebec River. Unlike most of the rivers we have had to ford, the Kennebec is impossible to cross on foot. From bank to bank, it stretches almost 400 feet and has a very strong and deep current. I am not sure exactly how deep it is, but I'm sure it is too deep to stand! Not even the fabled Gizmo wished to test it.

The official AT route involves the use of a ferry from one side to the other. This "ferry", which is no more than guy in a canoe taking hikers across in pairs, is notorious for long lines and delays. It is for this reason we got an early start and arrived at the riverbank as quickly as possible.

Our ferry man was quite a muscular fellow, and his jolly demeanor was contagious. He loaded us unto his canoe one at a time without delay. I soon found out why he was so muscular - due to the current he had to take us about 50 yards upriver along the bank before turning to cross. Despite what I would imagine to be quite the workout, he talked and joked almost the entire way across the rushing river. We ended up on the other side directly across from where we started. I tipped the man $10 for services well rendered.

Just a short walk from the mighty Kennebec is US 201, a paved road that, when followed, takes you into a town called Caratunk. Gizmo needed to stop by Northern Outdoors for some supplies, and since Aeriel really wanted to continue hanging out with him, we joined for the fun. As it turns out, I am really glad we did! Northern Outdoors is much more than just an Outfitters as I originally thought. It is an entire resort. I'm talking showers, hot tubs, restaurants, laundry, even a brewery! It was hiker heaven.

I didn't join in with the hot tubs, but I did take the opportunity to shower and play a few games of Galaga in their small arcade! At the restaurant I got a philly cheese steak roll, six hot wings, onion rings, and a huge brownie sunday handmade by our cute waitress. I could have eaten twice as much but, unfortunately, didn't have the money. This is certainly the kind of place I would like to come back to!

It was hard leaving Caratunk, but we have miles to go yet! So, with clean bodies and full stomachs we hitched back to the trail and set foot once again into wilderness. We walked about 12 more miles and made our camp at a site just past Moxie Pond and Baker Stream. We are still hiking along with Gizmo, who has proved to be an excellent companion, and will probably stick with us until Katahdin. Aeriel offered him a ride from the northern terminus to wherever he needs to go!

All in all, it was a good day, full of adventure and memories.

Part 5

The 100 Mile Wilderness

Wednesday, July 9th
Day 27

A Hiker Fridge in Monson
-

Monson Maine is a beautiful little lake town tucked away in the wilderness. Despite its small size, it is a perfect place and holds special significance to AT Thru-Hikers in particular. Monson is the last easily accessible town before Katahdin and Baxter state park. Between us and the end of this portion of our journey is 100 miles of untamed wilderness. There will be no more paved roads, no more resupplies, and no more hostels until the end: a somewhat unnerving but exciting thought.

Our hike into town was beautiful and uneventful, we forded 3 different rivers and climbed up Moxie-Bald mountain. Maine is famous for a soda called Moxie and hiking up this mountain definitely put me in the mood for some! In town we decided to stay at Shaw's Hostel, a beautiful two-story white house that offers bunks, food, gear, a decent resupply, and anything else that may be needed by an adventurer about to cross 100 miles of wilderness.

One of Shaw's Hostel's more distinguishing features is its "hiker fridge". The hiker fridge is an old thing faded with age and plastered with outdoorsy stickers. It is free to use during your stay. You can put beer in there to enjoy during your say, extra food from a local restaurant, or anything else you may want to keep cold during your visit. Being the ravenous thru-hiker that I apparently am, I looked through the fridge and discovered an untouched pulled pork sandwich wrapped in tin-foil. This sandwich looked great, but being the kindhearted soul that I am, and not wanting to steal another hikers' food, I left it. It was tempting though!!

Aeriel stayed up especially late hanging out with Gizmo and drinking beer. I did not partake, deciding instead to spend some alone time with my journal. I am also hoping to get some extra sleep before heading out tomorrow. I am super excited for the "100 Mile Wilderness" and Katahdin!!

Thursday, July 10th
Day 28

A Terrible, Awful, Very Bad Decision
-

Today didn't start out as a terrible, awful, very bad day, but it soon became one. Leaving Monson was an interesting mixture of excitement and nervousness. We were taking our first steps into the "100 Mile Wilderness". At this point we have come quite a long way already and our "trail legs" are well developed, so we didn't figure we would have any issues.

Getting back into the Maine woods felt comfortable, the tall trees and green underbrush welcomed us with what seemed like a warm embrace. Even the mud and the cloud of mosquitos that followed me about didn't seem so bad.

Around mile 8 though, something happened. There was a slight twinge in my stomach. It didn't feel bad, at first, but over the course of the next hour that twinge built up into a pain, and that pain turned into something much more malignant. I needed to go.

That was my first poop of the day but it certainly wouldn't be my last. I am sorry to report, but there were no solid bits in there whatsoever. Shortly thereafter I threw up.

Again, it would not be for the last time. I guess there may have been something wrong with that pulled pork sandwich I snagged from the hiker-fridge this morning…

As it turns out, eating mysterious sandwiches from old and faded hiker fridges may not be the best thing to do. I just couldn't help it! It was there, it was beautiful, it looked so good and, because we were the last ones in the hostel, I knew that someone had left it by accident! It would have been a shame to leave such wonderful calories alone to rot… Apparently though, it already had.

We continued our journey, each step feeling as if it may be my last. As it became clear to my sister and I that my food poisoning wasn't going anywhere soon we briefly considered turning back to Monson. This (probably smarter) idea was tossed out though because neither of us wanted to walk 10 miles in the wrong direction. We decided to stay where we were and make camp.

I've been up all night at this point. In almost exactly 10-minute intervals I have to get out of my hammock to either throw up, or deal with explosive diarrhea. I tried to eat some ramen, but that made it about 2 mins before coming right back up again. I stopped zipping up the bug net on my hammock after it got caught up and almost caused me to throw up inside my sleeping bag.

I'm writing this at 4AM, and I feel absolutely shitty. I have gotten no sleep, I can't eat, and even what little water I try to drink comes right back up again. I am doing my best to drink as much as possible though, the last thing I want to be out here is dehydrated.

This is the worst food poisoning of my life.

It is what it is.

Friday, July 11th
Day 29

Squelch Buttons

This morning I was not feeling any better, I had gotten maybe a total of two hours of sleep last night and I still couldn't eat. Aeriel and I decided that we needed to push through in order to keep from falling behind. Neither of us wanted to turn around back to Monson, and we couldn't stay where we were for another day or we would run the risk of depleting our food stores before making it the 90 more miles to the next supply point. So onward we went! I had Aeriel go on in front of me because I wanted to go my own slow pace and didn't want to deal with other people while feeling so bad.

About halfway up the climb to Barren Mountain my miserable solitude was interrupted by some increasingly loud voices coming up from behind me… I could especially hear one particularly annoying voice complaining about a "squelch button" on his radio. I'm not sure what a squelch button is, but its not something I want to hear about in high volume and in a squeaky voice in my current condition. A few minutes later my horrible morning and horrible climb got worse as a family of self-proclaimed missionaries (I guess Maine needs missionaries?) appeared behind me and started to bombard me with questions in incredibly loud voices. There were a whole bunch of them, a dad, a grandfather, a mother, and a son. It seemed as if they there babbling about nonstop with infinite energy. I know they were just trying to be nice and talkative, but I was NOT in the mood.

I'm not sure if it was my super pale face, or if it was me informing them about my night of explosive diarrhea, but they eventually got the idea that I didn't feel like doing much talking and continued up the mountain in front of me still complaining about squelch buttons into their radio. They were kind enough to offer me some Powerade though, which actually made me feel a LOT better. Aeriel later informed me that when they caught up to her on the top of the mountain, they berated her for leaving me behind. HAHA!

To all the Maine missionaries out there: you're nice people, albeit a bit pretentious, and thanks for the Powerade.

As the day progressed, I slowly began to feel better and better, and despite my slow start we were still able to make about 20 miles total to the base of White Cap Mountain.

Saturday, July 12th
Day 30

Life is Like a River
-

I suppose life is like a river, there are times it is smooth and slow flowing, where you glide along enjoying every minute of it. Then there are times of rapids and turmoil, where you are tossed and thrown about without reprieve. You start off as a small spring trickling between two rocks and as you grow the distinctions between those calms and rapids becomes only clearer. Sometimes you can't see around the next bend; you don't know what is coming next. But one thing is for sure: you will get past it, life will flow on, it always does.

Life is like a river, and real life is backpacking.

Sunday, July 13th
Day 31

Antler Campsite Reflections
-

It is my one-month mark! It's awesome! It doesn't feel like a month, but at the same time it feels like a year... I don't know!! The trail is the only place I have ever been where every moment I look back on I remember as exactly the right amount of time. Things don't go by too quickly, and things don't seem to go by too slowly. It's as if time seems exactly right out here.

I've been quite down the last few days. I'm not sure exactly why, but it all started with my food poisoning incident. I do feel as if it's important to notice the moments in life where you aren't feeling the best. It adds much needed dimension and helps one better appreciate the good. Yesterday, we hiked over White Cap Mountain and got our first good look at Katahdin from a distance. I was in a special kind of funk, so I didn't write much.

Katahdin isn't the end for me, as it is for many of those I have met, but it is certainly something. It's peak towers above the surrounding forests like a lonely sentry protecting the north from further incursion. Two more days, then I will be conquering that mighty mountain!

Today we had planned to traverse 25 miles of the Maine wilderness, but our plans fell to the wayside as we discovered the magical Antler Campsite. Situated on the side of lake in a sort of peninsula, there is a wonderful breeze and no bugs. I'm not sure how or why, but the lack of mosquitoes buzzing and dive-bombing my ears was noticeable almost as soon as we entered the camp. The beauty and peace of the place was too much to pass up, so we set up and settled in for an afternoon and evening of relaxation.

A peaceful and beautiful place seems the perfect opportunity to try and re-center myself and reattain my baseline happiness. I have found that some places create the perfect atmosphere for self-reflection and self-exploration. This is one of those places.

I imagine that people become sad for many reasons. A loss, a disappointment, or anything else. But why am I feeling this way? What caused it, and what can I do to gain an acceptance of it? I feel like more people should focus on knowing themselves. We often run around the world feeling what we feel and thinking what we think without as much as a single thought dedicated to WHY we feel what we feel and WHY we think what we think.

Many people are depressed, and many are sad. Even amongst the beauty of nature I am feeling these things. Out here, at least, I have the time to feel and think them through. This is a luxury that many in their busy lives probably don't even realize they need. For almost all human history this never would have been an issue. But now, even our downtime is filled with screens and distractions. I will keep that in mind when I return.

This, I believe, is the secret to the calming and elating nature of the wilderness. It isn't just the trees, the green, the quiet, and the peace (although I imagine those things play their part); it is the exploration of your own mind that naturally occurs in the moments where you have nothing to do. It is easy to get those moments out here. Much more so than in our technologically crazed lives.

Sometimes the forced self-reflection out here can be too much. Some, maybe all, gaze into their own minds and are frightened by what they find.

Monday, July 14th
Day 32

One-Hundred Thousand Screaming Girls
-

For supposedly being one of the more remote sections of the AT, the 100-mile wilderness certainly has lots of people. We keep running into these "adventure groups" of some kind that take people out and introduce them to backpacking. As much as I like the idea of introducing people to backpacking, it's certainly annoying for me. They are very loud and very slow moving. Every time we catch up to one of the groups, we inevitably get stuck behind them and are forced to annoyingly announce ourselves and our intent to pass before the leader realizes we are there and gets everyone to step aside! Perhaps I am too harsh.

We did another 25-mile day today starting at Antler Campsite and ending at Rainbow Spring Campsite. The lakes here are certainly beautiful, and I understand why they would attract lots of people. The only real up-hill climb we had to do today was Nesuntabunt Mountain which, after all the recent flat, seemed very difficult despite being less than 1000 feet of incline. It was, however, incredibly beautiful. Over-looking miles and miles of forests, lakes, and hills from its summit produced a wholly unique feeling that I cannot fully describe. One group we passed ate lunch at the top, a good choice!

We are sharing our campsite today with a group of what seems to be one-hundred thousand screaming girls all between the ages of 12 and 15… it seems the serene peace of the wilderness was not meant to last forever… All in all, a good day.

Tuesday, July 15th
Day 33

For Me, Acceptance
-

Today we woke up and left camp before 6 o'clock: the earliest we have ever done. Dad would be proud! We hiked the remaining 10 miles of the 100-mile wilderness and emerged from the woods onto a dirt road leading to a small convenience store and restaurant – the first opportunity we have had for real food and supplies since we left Monson. The gasoline was priced at $4.75 a gallon and everything in the convenience store was equally over-priced. Oddly enough, however, the pricing of the restaurant food was incredibly reasonable. Naturally, Aeriel, Gizmo, and I (and a few others we met along the way) took advantage. I ordered a BLT with the fries and, once learning of the unique wonders of these fries, then proceeded to order another huge plate of them for $5. The best $5 I have spent in a looooonngggg time! I also got to flirt with the waitress, that was fun!

The next 10 miles into Baxter State Park and to the base of Katahdin seemed to fly by. Grey clouds moved in overhead pairing well with the happy-sad feelings my companions must have been experiencing in view of the end. For me, Katahdin is not the end. For me it is an acceptance. An acceptance into the wilderness and an acceptance into the lifestyle of a backpacker. Unlike Gizmo, I still have many, many more miles to travel before my end, yet I cannot help getting caught up into the general mood of wonder, excitement, shock, and sadness of a lofty goal accomplished.

We made it to Baxter and to Birches campsite. We are now at the base of what is both the largest mountain in Maine and the end of the first major portion of my journey. We registered at the Ranger's office (who was a cool guy to talk to) and returned to camp. The dark clouds still show no sign of abating. KATAHDIN TOMORROW!!! RAIN OR SHINE!!

Tuesday, July 16th
Day 34

Summiting Katahdin
-

I do believe that we must be cursed! Every time we are supposed to climb a major mountain the fog, the rain, and the clouds move in and obscure what are supposed to be some of the greatest and most awe-inspiring views of the Appalachian Trail.

We woke up early this morning for our Katahdin ascent, and we could tell almost immediately that the weather would not be cooperating with us. The skies were overcast and looking up toward the mountain did not reveal its rugged and rocky peak, but instead a swirling and misty mass of clouds, fog, and rain. Despite this, upward we went.

For Aeriel, Gizmo, and I, our assent was marked with an air of excitement and shock. For Gizmo, these were his last steps of a many month adventure that has seen him from the very tip of Florida to the most northern part of the Continental United States. For Aeriel and I, this climb represented not only the completion of the first stage of our journey, but also something deeper that would come to define us as individuals.

The climb up Katahdin was a very tough one. There were moments we had to climb hand over hand up boulders and across steep drop-offs. Occasionally, the fog thinned enough so that we could see out toward the wilderness from which we had hiked, but as we ascended further the fog and drizzle became thicker and we were drowned by a sea of grey.

On our final approach to the summit, Gizmo stripped down to only his underwear and utility belt (he promised himself that he would summit Katahdin in such a manner) and climbed the rest of the way through the cold rain and fog mostly naked. When the renowned summit sign came into view, he ran to it, embraced it as an old friend, and shouted a glorious and victorious yell. I am honored that I could witness and be a part of the fulfillment of his journey. I can only imagine exactly what he was feeling in those moments, but I am sure those thoughts were a confusing mixture of shock, sadness, happiness, joy, sorrow, and very well-earned sense of pride in his accomplishment.

On our descent I became more and more filled with a sense of intoxicating excitement for the rest of my southbound journey along this astounding path. What other sights were left for me to see? Who were the people that I would be destined to meet? What kind of stories would I walk away with? And what more would I learn about myself and my abilities? Only time will tell...

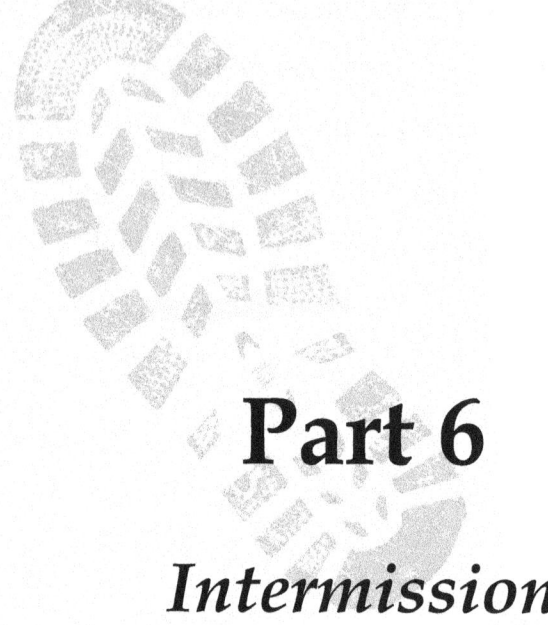

Part 6

Intermission

Days 35 – 38

Finishing Vermont

After Katahdin, we spent a day with Uncle Gary and Aunt Sarah just relaxing, eating, reading, and taking a wonderful break. Aunt Sarah dropped us off at Route 4 in Vermont around 9:30 AM so that we could pick up the section Aeriel had skipped. My father had convinced her to jump over the first half of Vermont because he had already done that portion of the trail when he was in college.

So, the next few days were spent hiking as fast as we could to finish the section between VT Route 4 and VT Route 9. We had to leave soon for a family reunion on the beach in North Carolina, and Aeriel didn't want to leave any bit of northern trail unfinished! I didn't write much in my journal during this time, but we met all kids of interesting individuals! The section wasn't too long, and we finished it up in 3 days! A great time!

I am sitting at Gram's and Gramp's house right now. After we finished Aeriel's last section in the north, we were picked up by Gary once again. He brought us back to his house where we enjoyed a steak dinner and ICE cream.

Cold foods and Ice cream are especially wonderful after being out in the wilderness for so long! Refrigeration is just another one of those things that we take for granted in everyday life. It is crazy to think that having cold foods constantly on hand is a modern phenomenon.

Gary drove us to Gram's and Gramp's house to spend some time with them before heading to NC tomorrow evening.

So far on the AT I've walked about 578 miles in 37 walking days. I don't think that's too bad! 😊 I am really looking forward to heading back to the Delaware Water Gap and the Appalachian Trail after some wonderful rest. It won't be too long before we are back in the woods and are climbing mountains once again!

As it is planned right now, our first day back on the trail will be August 3rd. I will be back!!

At The Beach

Inspired by the Duality of the Sea and Mind
-

The tide is going. Like what hope is left inside me, it is fleeting. Not quickly, necessarily, but consistently. The warmer sand feels soft on my calloused feet, reminding me of my soft and carefree past. It contrasts sharply with the wind blowing briskly from the sea carrying with it salty tears which dampen my now heavy soul.

Clouds are rolling in the distance separating indefinitely the starlit sky into two: the good and the evil, that is the old and the new. The lightning momentarily brightens the darkened day.

I am walking now, unstopped, seemingly unnoticed into the unceasing, never stilled, ocean which is eternity. And in doing so I am untethered myself from the norm and cutting the umbilical cord which has sustained me thus far.

I go in, never to come out. I go in, into the unknown – loving it.

- Inspired by the Duality of the Sea and Mind

The way I see it, life is a lot like the night sky. Mostly its dark, bland, boring: work and tiresome people.

Occasionally, though, it is broken up by beautiful shiny lights which gleam like holes in the floor of heaven. It is for those bright, and perfect moments you must live for in life. You must strive to make those moments more bight and more plentiful. It is a struggle we all face.

Much like how you can drive to the country and see a clearer sky, you can also put yourself into positions in life where your sky has a brighter and a more glorious disposition.

Part 7

A New SOBO Start

Sunday, August 3rd
Day 39

No need to Rush
-

Today Auntie S and Uncle G dropped us off at the Delaware Water Gap at around 10:30AM. It feels so good to be back on the trail! The past week was spent relaxing on a North Carolina beach and eating all the food I could. It was truly glorious. Even Gizmo stopped by to say hi!

Our first steps heading south-bound on the trail consisted of a 1000ft uphill climb onto a ridge that we will be staying on for basically all of Pennsylvania. The climb was tough after a week of relaxation, but my trail legs eventually got back into it! We hiked about 6 miles and found a shelter where we decided to take our lunch break. But, having nowhere specific to be and wanting to break ourselves back into the trail slowly, we decided to stay the whole night. We have a lot of time to get to the end of the trail at Springer Mountain and have no real need to rush!

We met a lot of interesting people passing through the shelter. Most of all of them were north- bounders heading to Maine! When I started in Vermont we were ahead of the main group of North Bounders (referred to as the "Bubble"). Now, we are heading south and are ahead most of all the SOBOs. I'm sure we will see, and possibly hike with, a few of them. It's too bad that most are behind.

I think that deciding to "Flip-Flop" the trail in the way we are was a really good idea of my sister's. We are hitting all the best places at the right times. We are also going to be hiking with significantly fewer people. You may think this is a bad thing, but the AT can certainly get crowded. I imagine that being around all the people could get quite miserable at times.

A NOBO named Sonic is staying with us at the shelter tonight and we discussed the trail ahead for her, our experiences with the White Mountains and Vermont, as well as her experience with Pennsylvania and everything south! We had heard a lot about the terrible Pennsylvania rocks, and Sonic confirmed that PA is filled with fields of boulders and fist-sized rocks to twist our ankles on. Can't wait!

Monday, August 4th
Day 40

The PA Rocks!
-

Yesterday we decided to take it easy. Today, not so much! We hiked a total of 19.8 miles through the PA rocks I've heard so much about. I don't think they have stood up to their terrible reputation. I haven't had any issues with my feet yet. Aeriel, on the other hand, disagrees. She is starting to have some issues with their effect on her feet. Her boots are pretty worn out, and the sharp rocks are putting pressure in unusual spots. It helps that the terrain is all flat, we both feel as if we can walk forever!

About 13 miles into our day, we stopped at Leroy Shelter for lunch where The Professor, Thumper, and Zeek (three south-bounders we have met previously) passed us. I'm sure we will see them again! We also saw a few more NOBOs as well, including a cute girl wearing a faded pink hat! I bet any cute girls I see will be heading the wrong way ☹.

The heat today, while not overly overbearing, was not particularly fun. It's quite different than the alpine forests of the north. We are camping tonight without water because the spring at the shelter is dry.

This is the first time on the entire trip so far where we need water but are not able to get any. My experience thus far has been one of liquid abundance. In the north we were basically tripping over the stuff. But, we are in the south now and are walking into the heat of the summer. Forgetting that could lead to major problems. We will not let it happen again!

We are running very low on water and have 10 miles to go tomorrow before our next source… not fun. We decided that it would be best not to cook dinner tonight to save what little water we have left for tomorrow. A hiker named Hatchet and his dad are camping with us and are in the same waterless boat.

Tuesday, August 5th
Day 41

Saved by the Waffle
-

My goodness... Where do I start for today???
This morning we woke up and started our 10-mile hike to the next water source. As the sun rose in the sky, the temperature rose with it. It soon became apparent that we would NOT have enough water to make it. After 4 miles I had already ran out and was thirsty. I stopped at a road crossing to wait for Aeriel and, when she caught up, I learned that she too had run out. Not wanting to walk another 6 miles through the summer heat with no water, we opted to walk down the road in hopes of finding someone or something that could help us.

At first, there was nothing but forest and trees, but very quickly we started to see houses and clearings. In less than a mile from the trail we found a small breakfast diner. What luck!!

Stopping at this restaurant ended up being one of the best decisions I think we have ever made. We only wanted to fill up our water, but the amazing smells enticed us to enter and sit. I ended up ordering a waffle. This waffle was delightfully fluffy and was sprinkled with powdered sugar. It was most definitely the best waffle I have ever eaten. The ice-cream I ordered for desert was also quite wonderful. After our meal, we refilled on water (and got some extra for Hatchet and his dad) and got a ride back to the trail with a nice couple we had met.

The next six miles to the next water source were hot and NOT shady at all. It was good that we had stopped at the restaurant because we would have been in bad shape if we had not! We found Hatchet and his dad a few miles down the trail foraging for berries and anything else they could use to find a bit of moisture. We readily shared our extra water which we had brought for the purpose. They were quite grateful!

We all ended up getting to the next spring alive, but the experience stood as a stark reminder that we are still in the wilderness and that anything could happen. Today we were lucky, we were saved by a waffle. We learned our lesson.

Today we ended up walking a total of 21.4 miles and are now camped at a powerline. The wind is bad and Aeriel and I both feel as if there is a storm on its way.

Wednesday, August 6th
Day 42

Settling In

Today was another strange PA day. Nothing strange actually happened, but there is just something about Pennsylvania. It's weird. We are hiking along a single very large ridge, and we only descend from it to go into towns or because there is a road crossing. There are pretty areas for sure but, for the most part, it seems to be a very unimpressive state. Just the same ol' rocks, trees, and heat. My least favorite state along the trail so far.

Today was another 20+ mile day and, although I was present for the entirety, it feels like it just sort of happened without excitement. We are just trying to get the miles done.

I'm not bored, nor am I sad. In fact, quite the opposite. I am excited to be here and every day I wake up excited. I wouldn't want to be anywhere else in the world. There seems as if there is just a settling in of sorts. We have many miles left to travel and not all those miles can be in the wildernesses of Vermont, New Hampshire, and Maine.

Tomorrow we are going into town called Hamburg. This will be our first resupply since getting back on the trail!

There is a Walmart and An AYCE Chinese place! I doubt that Aeriel will need much convincing to stop by for a hefty lunch! Haha!

Thursday, August 7th
Day 43

Curious Planting Habits of PA Farmers
-

So, you know how they talk about people getting lost in corn fields? Well, I don't know about you, but I never thought it was the kind of thing that *actually* happens. I mean, who gets lost in corn fields, right? Apparently, we do.

We walked down from our Pennsylvania ridge to Highway 61 into Hamburg without issue. Traffic was moving very quickly and it was not a good place to get a hitch, so we decided to walk the 1.5 miles into town.

About half-way down the road we could see the Walmart sitting, in all of its wonderful glory, on top of a distant hill. It was separated from us by a small cornfield nestled in a beautiful little valley. Why not cut through the cornfield and save us quite a bit of time? Well, Aeriel thought this to be a great idea and convinced me of the same. So, down the hill and into the field we went.

We chose a row and began walking. You can never really tell just how tall corn grows until you are under and surrounded by it. It grew up above us by at least a good 2 or 3 feet. The heat between all the stalks was stifling, but the experience was a new one for me and was quite enjoyable at first. We never strayed from our chosen row of corn, but as we walked, and walked, and walked, and kept on walking, the heat began to get to us. Sweat poured down my face and small particles of dust and chaff stuck to me like bacon grease on a pan. We continued on for what seemed like a good bit of time, too much time. The field certainly didn't look that big from our vantage point on the highway...

Eventually, we popped out of the field on what we assumed was the other side, except there was no Walmart and there was no highway. It was as if we had stepped through an invisible portal of corn and were thrown back into a time before thoughts of such things were even conceived. Needless to say, we were both confused and disoriented. Instead of taking the risk of getting lost further, we decided to turn back and follow the same row of corn back to where we came from. So, we did. Sure enough, what seemed like ages later we popped back out from the field covered in silt and sweat in full view of the highway and the Walmart on the hill. What the heck?

We climbed back up to the highway, confused about what had happened. It was only when we were able to see the cornfield from a distance once again that we realized our mistake. The corn was not planted in straight rows like we had assumed. Instead, it had been planted in large, rounded rows in the shape of a semi-circle. Where we had come out of the field was on the same side that we had entered, only on the other end. There were no magic portals at work, only the curious planting habits of Pennsylvania Farmers…

We finished our walk on the road and, once we did finally get the Walmart, we ate lunch and resupplied. I bought an awesome calculator watch! We got back to the trail in the late afternoon and hiked another 8.2 miles to Eagles Nest Shelter for the Evening.

Friday, August 10th
Day 44

Grizzly Grouse
-

Grouse are odd creatures. Sort of a mix between chickens and turkeys, but smaller. These birds hang out on the ground and, when startled, will take off like Apache Attack Helicopters flying directly at the face of the person or animal who startled them. They do this to distract any potential predators from noticing and eating their young. This is both an interesting survival method and a terrifying experience for those of us who are the victims of this procedure.

Grizzly Grouse is an interesting chap. Hiking southbound in sandals and sporting a scraggly beard, he seems both of the woods and just visitor. Grizzly Grouse got the second half of his name from an incident he had with one. Apparently, he startled it and, instead of ducking when it charged for his head, instinctually swung his arm and punched it out of the sky. He killed it quite by accident. Instead of wasting the bird, he tied it to his pack and continued hiking (this gained him lots of attention from those he passed by). That night he plucked the feathers, cleaned it, and had himself a wonderfully fire roasted grouse. A well-deserved trail name if I've ever heard one.

We met Grizzly Grouse at around lunch time and walked with him for a bit chatting about our experiences. He was a pleasant companion and joined us at 501 Shelter for the evening. 501 Shelter is a wonderful place and comes complete with an outdoor shower fed by collected rain, a large collection of books to read, as well as access to a road if you would like to order pizza! Aeriel and I decided that this shelter must be a "god shelter." I found a book about Buddhist meditation that I found most enlightening.

We also met a guy named Color Bandit here. Color Bandit is a sort of trail celebrity due to his habit of coloring in illustrations left in the logbooks by another hiker. Both are incredibly talented, and their works of art are amazing.

There are many such logbooks on the trail where hikers check in and can see who is in front of them. It's a great system for keeping up with others and for learning of news and situations that may affect you. Often, hikers also write of their thoughts, feelings, and experiences along the trail.

Saturday, August 9th
Day 45

Stories, Now Forgotten
-

The United States of America is an enchanting place. It fascinates me to consider the lives of its earliest settlers. At a time when this place truly was a wilderness, they lived here. In amongst these trees and hills that I now walk through, they lived and died. What experiences and memories did they have? What loves? What joys and what sadnesses did they experience here?

As we walked on we began to see the remains of old buildings and stone structures: the ruins of a mining town. We found an old forgotten cemetery in the woods, a relic of a time forgotten. The inscription on one of the stones told of a 30-year-old man who died accidentally at Gold Mine Gap in 1856. The trees and underbrush are now the only settlers of this town, but I can't help thinking of what it must have been like all those years ago.

This area of PA is wonderful. Its thoughtful, its old, and the relics of the ages tell the most intriguing of stories. We walked 20 miles today and ended just past "The General": a steam engine that had been abandoned in the woods. It was left and forgotten; a rusting corpse from an age buried by time. What forgotten stories did it hide in its rusting corpse? We may never know.

Sunday, August 10th
Day 46

Into Duncannon
-

Today we hiked one of our highest mile days yet! 26 miles! That is a full marathon! Despite the distance, the day was very much uneventful except for an odd character we met who was out studying snakes. I believe he was a part of a conservation group in the area. We ran into him about 4 or 5 miles from Duncannon and he pointed out three copperhead snakes he had found who were hiding under some rocks on a ledge. He told us of their behavior and their migration and hunting patters. He was interesting and was a blast to talk to!

The Doyle Hotel is a thru-hiker must stop location. Not because its nice (its not), but because it's a tradition. This hotel is nestled in the embrace of downtown Duncannon, and walking into its ancient and creaky doorway was like walking through a portal into a haunted time capsule from the early 1900's. This three-story hotel was re-built after the original dating back to the 1700s burnt down. Today, it is a dirty, leaning, creaky, leaky, but absolutely amazing hotel. We weren't able to try the food because they had already closed the kitchen for the evening, but our room was located on the corner of the building on the 3rd floor next to the fire escape (which is good because I feel like the building could collapse at any moment).

For dinner we got pizza, music, and good memories at Sorrento's Pizza and Bar. It was a great place, and I imagine that it was a lot cleaner than the kitchen at the Doyle.

Monday, August 11th
Day 47

Thanks Spock!
-

I woke up before Aeriel this morning and decided to get our laundry done at the local laundromat. While I was waiting for the layers and layers of dust, dirt, and grime to be washed off I decided to stop by a place called Goodies for breakfast. Being in a outgoing and talkative mood, I struck up a conversation with this guy who was about my age and his dad at the next table. They were nice and ended up picking up my tab for me! The kindness of strangers continues to surprise me.

Speaking of the kindness of strangers, we met up with Spock again! We had contacted him awhile back and he drove the 20 or 30 minutes from his house to come say, "hi", and take us out to eat. He drove us to a neighboring town called Carlisle for lunch at a place called Bruges. Carlisle seems like the younger, better looking, and more successful brother of Duncannon. It's certainly much more posh.

For lunch, Spock treated us to the most amazing muscles. I've had oysters and clams before, but never muscles! I suppose I just have never had the chance before; thank you Spock! I'm happy he came out to see us. It was nice to take the day to relax and enjoy ourselves.

After resupplying at a local grocery store, we hit the trail once again. Spock tagged along for the first 4 miles up to the next shelter and then said goodbye. He was excited to hike a few miles on the trail, I think he misses it. I saw another rattlesnake on our way up! This was the second one I have seen since starting back up; apparently snakes like PA!

Tuesday, August 12th
Day 48

Farmlands
-

As mentioned in previous entries, hiking in Pennsylvania consists mostly of rock scrambling on a flat ridgeline. Today, however, we got something different. Today we hiked off the ridgeline not for a road crossing or a town, but to traverse almost 15 miles of flat fields and farmland. How wonderful.

Hiking off the mountain ridge and descending into this expanse of flat farmland was beautiful and tranquil. It was made more intense by a heavy fog that descended upon us like a wool blanket. It rained sporadically throughout the day which added another dynamic to the sensations and feelings of the experience. The farmland was flat and easy to walk along. The fog and overcast sky blotted out the sun which was quite refreshing. Most people, I imagine, would have to suffer the summer heat.

We saw Grizzly Grouse on and off today as well. It seems like we are going at about the same pace he is. Tomorrow we should hit the midpoint of the Appalachian

Trail, a huge landmark for us!! To think that in all this time we have only come halfway is crazy.

Still have lots of walking to do yet!

Wednesday August 13th
Day 49

The Half Gallon Challenge
-

The "Half-Gallon-Challenge" is a AT thru-hiker staple tradition. At right around the middle point of the trail there is a little convenience store that sells half-gallons of ice cream, and what better way to celebrate your accomplishment but to eat one? Half a gallon of ice cream to celebrate half the trail completed, makes sense to me!

Today was good, we had a later start than normal but still made decent time and got to the AT museum and midpoint. We met two hikers named Science-Tooth and Sparkly Pony. They were stragglers behind the main pack of NOBOs. It wouldn't surprise me if they would be the last ones we saw as they did not know of anyone behind them. Grizzly Grouse was also sitting at a picnic table when we arrived trying to decide if he wanted to attempt the half gallon challenge. Despite Aeriel's apprehensions (she did not partake), Grizzly Grouse and I decided that an attempt was a must!

Now, even for a food deprived thru-hiker, trying to down half a gallon of a sugary dairy product is quite the challenge. There was some discussion about what the best flavor to choose would be and about what the best method would be to get it all down. Apparently, some hikers would let the ice cream melt before *drinking* the half gallon. That approach made sense but sounded a bit like cheating and not near as much fun! Eventually, I decided to attempt the challenge with Mint Chocolate Chip (tastes better than vanilla and will hopefully go down just as easy) and a spoon. I am proud to admit that the challenge was a success for both Grizzly Grouse and myself! It's crazy the extreme backpackers will go to in the realm of food consumption.

Thursday, August 14th
Day 50

Cruising Through PA

Today we did 26 miles over some of the nicest terrain yet. Mostly, it was flat and there were very few rocks. The soft rolling fields were overtaken with grass and made for the perfect place for rabbits. We saw two this morning! We ate lunch at a powerline clearing that made for a decent view and met two musicians named Daniel and Steven. Daniel and Steven where only out for the week but were good people and fun to talk to. They were really interested in the details of our hike!

The shelters in this area are pretty. After lunch we passed one called "Quarry Gap Shelter" that was basically two shelters set side by side with about 10 to 15 feet between them with a roof over top. It made for a perfect place for picnic tables out of the sun and out of the rain. The "Tumbling Run Shelters," where we are at tonight, are also really nice. We met another SOBO and his dad as well. It's nice to know that we won't be completely alone hiking toward Georgia. We are planning a short day tomorrow before attempting something called the "4 State Challenge". More on that later though.

Aeriel just thought it best to inform me of her greatest regret on the AT so far… that she didn't try to see Gizmo naked at the Hiker Hut while he was bathing in the river… really, thanks for letting me know.

Friday, August 15th
Day 51

An Amazing Experience
-

I've said it before and I will say it again, the people you meet while thru-hiking are some of the best and nicest in the world. Aeriel and I took our time this morning getting out of camp (we are planning a very short and restful day before attempting the "4 State Challenge") and ended up going only 2 or 3 miles before stopping at PA Route 16 to eat some lunch.

While sitting beside the road in a parking area, a wonderful couple stopped to say, "hi", and talk to us. They gave us some left-over food they had from their breakfast and some candy. We talked for a while before they gave us their number and drove away. They told us to call if we needed anything.

5 – 10 minutes later the same couple came back and offered to let us stay the night at their house. Showers, food, beds, and relaxation before one of the toughest days of hiking we will have? Absolutely. I don't know what made these people decide to take us in for the evening, but they were AMAZING. Probably the nicest people we have met

so far. They bought us KFC on the way back to their house where we met their 13 dogs (we stopped at McDonalds to get each dog half of a burger) and were able to get a shower and do some relaxing.

And yes, you read that right. This couple has *13 Dogs*. Each dog gets half a cheeseburger from McDonalds once a week (I am not sure who gets the remaining half), gets homemade chicken for dinner every night - unless a special diet is needed, and is named after a Republican president. These people treat their dogs better than some people treat their kids. I am in awe.

Later that night we were joined by one of this couple's friends and were taken to a local fair that was going on. It was soooooo much fun!! They bought us food, let us play fair games (I won a ninja banana), introduced us to the local history, and refused to let us spend any money ourselves. I realize now that there is no real value in money except if you have fun and make memories spending it. The couple spent almost $300.00 on us today and gave us one of the best experiences of our lives. Truly amazing and wonderful people.

Tomorrow we start the 4-State Challenge…

Saturday, August 16th
Day 52

What is the 4-State Challenge??

Aeriel and I just woke up after what is probably the best night of sleep either of us have had for a while. We were both clean and had our own beds (which were super comfy). Later today we are going to be driven back to the trail where we will start the "4-State Challenge".

The 4-State Challenge is a popular test of will among AT hikers. We will be starting at PA Route 16, about 2.3 miles from the PA-Maryland border, from there we will hike the 40.6 miles through Maryland and will then cross over into West Virginia and Harpers Ferry. After getting to Harpers we will then walk 2.7 miles to finish just past the Virginia border. To complete the challenge all of this must be done in a continuous 24-hour period.

So, in total, we will be starting at around noon in Pennsylvania and will hike a total of 45.6 miles through the night finishing just inside Virginia hopefully before noon tomorrow. This is called the 4-State Challenge because you start in PA, hike through MD and WV, and end in VA. To finish, we need to average 1.9 miles per hour for the entire 24-hour period. Wish us luck!

Sunday, August 17th
Day 53

The 4-State Challenge
-

I can say, without a doubt, that I just went through one of the toughest experiences of my life. Both mentally and physically. The 4-State Challenge started off well enough, pretty much just normal hiking, but as the sun set it turned into a battle of will between hikers and trail. Twilight overtook us, and with the growing darkness came homogeneity. We were wading through a sea of darkness broken only by our headlamps illuminating the ground before us.

In the darkness everything becomes the same, the previous five miles interchangeable with the next five. No views, no people. Only the engulfing darkness and two small patches of illuminated ground seeming to lead the way. Time itself seemed to meld itself together in our minds as well; what seemed like 20 minutes could have been 60 or it could have been only 5, we could not tell, we simply walked on.

At some point our minds, exacerbated by lack of sleep, became somewhat delirious. Calculating the miles remaining became a mental feat and we often misjudged. This added to the general mood of confusion and delirium. At one point we calculated that we had 14 miles to go when in reality we had 24. You can imagine my surprise and frustration when learning that, after 2 hours of walking, our "14 miles to go" turned into, "Oh shit, I think we still have 20 miles left."

I also had problems with my watch. Problems that, under normal circumstances, would be an easy fix. But because my tired brain didn't realize the problem had occurred, caused us to go 4 or 5 hours thinking we had walked a lot longer than we actually had. At around the 10 miles to go mark we downed two 5 Hour Energies we had brought (it didn't hit Aeriel too well, she spent about 20 minutes laughing like a crazy woman) and walked on.

The last stretch was the worst. It seemed to take forever. We walked up and down mountains, and then up and down some more. Seemingly not moving at all. Eventually, dawn began to break. The darkness that had swallowed us faded into the paleness of the early morning hours. We walked on.

We finished at the Virginia border at around 8:35AM. The whole challenge took us only 20 hours and 35 minutes yet had felt like an eternity. We crashed right past the sign welcoming us into Virginia and slept on the ground next to the trail for a handful of hours.

After we woke, we walked the 2.7 miles backwards to Harper's Ferry. We are planning to meet up with Aeriel's college friend Cameron who is planning to hike the first week or two of Virginia with us. It should be fun hiking with someone else again, even if its just for a short time!

The 4-State Challenge was a smashing success and, though mentally and physically taxing, it was an experience that tested the true limits of my endurance and one that I would not have wanted to miss.

Part 8
Enter Cameron

Monday, August 18th
Day 54

Continuing Cam's AT Adventure
-

Most of today was spent in Harpers Ferry recovering and helping Cameron figure out his first resupply. Harpers Ferry is a beautiful little town with history stretching back to the very beginnings of America. It was a pleasure walking it's old and narrow cobblestone streets and learning of it's civil war history.

Cameron had hiked with Aeriel and my dad during the first few weeks of the AT before I had joined on. And, as it turns out, he is planning on getting in a few more weeks before heading back to grad school! It will certainly be interesting hiking with someone else again. We are planning to go somewhat slow for the next few days so that he can get back in shape. This is fine by me! I could use a few days of rest!

We left Harpers in the afternoon and walked only four miles to a campsite we decided to call "The Glade". The Glade was right next to the road and, according to our guidebook, there was a gas station just a short walk away. Aeriel and Cameron decided to go buy a twelve pack of

Rolling Rock beers to celebrate the continuation of Cam's AT adventure.

Aeriel was pretty hesitant to give me any of the beer (she didn't want to get her young 16-year-old brother drunk). As it turns out, however, she has a lot more to fear from herself and Cameron than from me! Her tolerance must be completely shot. After only 3 beers each both Aeriel and Cameron were pretty far gone. I don't know how these two survived college.

I spent a few hours helping Aeriel survive throwing up by feeding her bread and drinking the rest of her beer (to help her avoid temptation!) I ended up drinking 6 total and was still much better off than either Aeriel or Cameron. I understand Aeriel's lack of tolerance, she has been out backpacking for the last three months, but what is Cameron's excuse?! He must just be a major lightweight. Hahaha!

Tuesday, August 19th
Day 55

Slow-Moving
-

Referring to our day today as "slow-moving" would be an understatement. Aeriel, Cameron and I took our sweet time packing up our things and getting out of camp this morning. We ended up walking only 3 miles to stay at David Lesser Memorial Shelter. I welcomed another slow day, but I do look forward to getting back up to the higher miles once Cam gets his trail legs!

I have never met Cameron before, and he is quite the interesting character. He is about my height (6 foot), lanky, has long dark hair pulled back into a ponytail, and sports a mid-length beard. His somewhat squinty eyes sit below bushy eyebrows and are complemented by clear, frameless glasses. He has a mostly cheery demeanor and seems like a nice enough fellow!

Virginia, so far, is quite nice. We have beautiful forests, well maintained trails, and the occasional view. Aeriel was telling me that about 800 miles (or just about a quarter) of the trail goes through Virginia and that its one of the toughest states on the mind. The "Virginia Blues" is a term used to describe the melancholy monotony people often feel trying to get through the state. Apparently, Virginia is the state where people tend to realize just how LOONG the AT really is… I'm not sure what to expect, but I know that I'm not going anywhere! I love it out here.

Our shelter for the night was another wonderful spot. We shared it with 4 other people who we hung out and played card games with. I even showed them some magic tricks! All in all, an uneventful day of low miles. Tomorrow should be better!

Wednesday, August 20th
Day 56

A Hostel for Cam

Today was a higher mile day than the last two, but still small comparatively. We walked 11 miles over mostly flat and downhill terrain. Cameron did alright considering that this was his first semi-long distance day!

Tonight we decided to stay at a hostel for Cam whose new trail name is *Rolling Rock*. We gave him the name due to his love of Rolling Rock Beer (as was made apparent a few nights ago). Our hostel for the night is quite a nice place! They have a TV so we watched Jurassic Park. I learned how to play the theme song on a guitar that they have here, that was fun!

I really like the hostels we have come across so far on the trail. Each is incredibly unique and has its own personality. Generally speaking, they are much cheaper than hotels and offer a much more relaxing environment to hang out with fellow hikers.

Thursday, August 21st
Day 57

A Worrying Amount of Aspirin

Ol' Cameron pops more aspirins than I think is healthy for him... haha. At the start of almost every uphill climb this guy insists on taking more and more to drown out the pain. He says that, since he is constantly walking and working out, his body can metabolize much more than the recommended daily dosage. I'm not so sure and am quite concerned. Pains while struggling up tough climbs are normal and I don't feel as if it is very smart to try and get rid of it completely. I have learned to listen to my body out here, to hear what the pains are telling me, and to adjust my movements accordingly. Drowning those pains with copious amounts of aspirin seems like a great way to hurt yourself in a much more serious way.

Today we woke up in the hostel and took our sweet time getting out. We took advantage of an amazing all-you-can-eat pancake b-fast and watched Grease on the TV. When we did finally hit the trail again, we started up the first hill in an area that is called the "Roller Coaster." The Roller Coaster is a stretch of about 10 miles where the trail goes up and down and up and down virtually endless amounts of little hills and mountains. Much like a roller coaster!

For Aeriel and I, these weren't so bad at first (although even I was pretty pooped by the end), but for Cameron they were hell on earth. There were moments that I am pretty sure he wanted to lay down and give up forever; if not for the worrying number of Aspirins he downed I think we would have lost him forever. I find myself doubting his mental fitness for something like long-distance backpacking.

In total we went the whole 10 miles of the Roller Coaster and finished at Rod Hollow Shelter. By the end Cameron was walking so slowly that I went on ahead by myself. I ended up waiting at the shelter for about 2 hours before Aeriel finally showed up with him! Aeriel says that he was the same way at the very beginning of the trail as well. She and my dad would have to wait hours for him to catch up!

Overall, we didn't get too many miles in for the day, but we started late and hiked over tough terrain with someone who just got back on the trail! All things considered we did very well.

Friday, August 22nd
Day 58

Fields of Grass and Flowers
-

Before Cam joined up with us, Aeriel and I were doing very well with getting out of camp early. Now, we are back to taking our time in the mornings! This is good and bad. On one hand, it's a more relaxing start to the day and allows for a more enjoyable pop-tart breakfast but, on the other hand, we typically are walking later into the evening and sometimes even have to do some night hiking. It's a give and take but, overall, I am okay with it!

We got out of the shelter around 10ish today and ended up hiking about 13 miles over a few decent mountains. It rained for a little bit but was honestly refreshing. We walked through this lovely area near Sky Meadows State Park that Aeriel says she recognized from a dream. It's a wonderful experience walking out from the woods and into beautiful fields of grass and flowers.

Tonight, we are staying at Manassas Gap Shelter where we ran into Connor again. I met Connor on my first or second night on the trail when we were heading NOBO and he was heading SOBO. I am glad to hear that he is still sticking with the trail and doing well! I am sure that, at our current pace, more and more south-bounders will catch up with us! I do hope so!

Saturday, August 23rd
Day 59

Into Front Royal

This morning started off much earlier than what is typical. We had decided to stay in the shelter last night with Connor. Well, at 5:30AM Connor's alarm went off, he sat up, downed a 5-hour energy, went back to sleep, woke up to another alarm at 6, then was packed up and gone by 6:15. Apparently, this is his normal morning time routine. He always sets an alarm 30 minutes before he wants to actually wake up so that he can drink his morning's 5-Hour Energy. He says that they take about 30 minutes to "fully take effect". Makes sense to me, I suppose.

This is one of the best and worst things about sleeping in shelters: other people. Inevitably, you are tied to their schedules. Waking up when the earliest riser gets up and starts packing. You can usually sleep through one or two people getting up but, when the shelter is crowded, one person packing up usually sets of a chain reaction of people moving around, packing, cooking, and altogether making a lot of noise!

Today we walked from our shelter to the road into Front Royal, about 10 miles or so. We got a hitch from a really nice lady who owns a hotel up the way. She dropped us off at a McDonalds where I got a Triple-Double. Which, for those of you who don't know, is three double cheeseburgers stacked on top of each other. Six patties full of wonderful goodness: the perfect meal for a hungry hiker! After McDonalds we resupplied at Martin's, a small grocery store across the street. Front Royal is another one of these small towns that I would love to come back to visit one day. Maybe even live in! There are so many interesting and beautiful places here along the AT.

After our resupply, we got a hitch out of Front Royal and hiked another 3 miles or so and ended our evening at Tom Floyd Shelter. We ended up doing a bit of night hiking up a mountain to get there. It was tiring and long after a resupply! All in all, we hiked about 14 or 15 miles today and were able to re-supply, a very good day of hiking! Cameron did well!

Sunday, August 24th
Day 60

Shenandoah National Park
-

We got another late start today. We didn't end up leaving camp until around Noon. I don't think we will be catching back up to Connor anytime soon considering his energy boosted early morning starts! The hike this morning started with the completion of Compton Peak and an entrance into Shenandoah National Park. The trail follows along Skyline Drive (a beautiful scenic drive which winds through the entirety of the Shenandoah Park) for about 100 miles. The AT crisscrosses with this road quite a few times and we should be able to see countless beautiful views! I am really looking forward to this portion of the trail!

There are apparently lots and lots of black bears in Shenandoah as well. Every shelter in the area has these bear poles to hang your food bags from, and we have heard lots of stories about hikers who have run into them in the area! I hope I get to see a few! You do have to be careful in these populated areas though. Many of the bears can get so used to people and people food that they are no longer scared and will come right up to you to try and get some. These kinds of situations can be very dangerous, and these bears will often end up having to be removed or killed if they become a problem. It is very unfortunate. Don't feed the bears people!!!

Aeriel told me of a bear encounter she and my dad had before I got on the trail. They were woken up in the middle of the night by a large black bear huffing around their camp. They yelled at it, banged pots and trekking poles, and tried their best to scare it off. It didn't care though, just meandered along through their campsite sniffing around and looking for food. Scary! Eventually, it wandered off on its own. I imagine that they may have had a major issue if the bear had smelt food in one of their tents.

The First 10 miles of SNP (Shenandoah National Park) were beautiful. We crossed Skyline Drive 4 or 5 times and got to see beautiful panoramic views each time we did so. There are lots of people in the park, but not as many as we actually expected, so that was nice! We hiked over North and South Marshal Mountain and eventually ended up and Gravel Springs Hut, our first shelter in SNP.

Yankee, a fellow SOBO we met, is at the shelter as well. We also met 4 boys who are out for the week, as well as a cute girl about my age who is out hiking with her dad, and a ridgerunner! A full house for tonight. Aeriel and I are camping outside of the shelter. We built a fire, and everyone hung out and shared stories of our experiences with the weekend and section hikers. We told of the rain, fog, and dangerous wind along Mount Washington, of the people we have met, and all the other crazy adventures we have had so far. I like to think that I may be inspiring future hikers. It was a ton of fun. I am really looking forward to tomorrow, the views are supposed to be really beautiful and there should be no rain!

Monday, August 25th
Day 61

Like an Animal in the Zoo

Today was the highest mile day we have gone since Ol' Cameron joined us on the trail! 17 miles! Cameron did well too. I think he is finally getting his trail legs. It helps that the trail in Shenandoah is very well maintained and quite nice. No roots, no mud, no crazy bushes taking over the trail, just easy walking! We definitely have some uphill climbs, but for the most part everything is easy going.

Occasionally, between two Skyline Drive crossings, I will run into some tour groups being led by rangers. They will stop us "Thru-Hikers" to let the tourists ask us questions. They look at us like we are animals in a zoo, and inevitably some small child will hide behind their mom or dad, but I quite like these encounters! The questions I get range from normal and mundane to incredibly dumb and humorous. Perhaps one of my favorites was, "Do you sleep?" No, random tourist, I have taken secret government pills that allow me to walk indefinitely forward in a constant dream-like state. Of course I sleep! Haha. I imagine that we thru-hikers must be quite the sight (and smell). I wonder if I inspired anyone to take on a similar journey? I hope so!

I haven't thought too much about what other people must think of someone doing a thru-hike. It's very interesting to consider. Most people probably don't realize that it is something that people do. Especially at my age! I always enjoy talking to people and seeing their reactions.

Today we hiked over Hogback Mountain, Pass Mountain, and eventually ended at Byrds Nest Shelter about halfway up Pinnacle Mountain. The views today were beautiful once again. Miles and miles of mountains, valleys, and forest stretched out before us, it was truly a wonderful feeling. Two SOBO hikers named Bear Snack and Copperhead Kid only made it to the shelter right before ours (we passed by them there). I have the feeling that we probably won't be seeing them again either, but who knows! We are sharing the shelter with a bunch of weekend and section hikers again tonight.

Tuesday, August 26th
Day 62

Sassafras
-

It feels really good to be climbing mountains again. Especially mountains overlooking such stunning views and scenery. I am loving Virginia so far and haven't had to deal with any "Virginia Blues" yet. I have also really enjoyed learning about a lot of the trees and plants we are walking by. My favorite is sassafras. Sassafras is a unique plant in that its leaves take on 3 very distinctive and unique shapes. Some of the leaves look like mittens, some look like little ghosts, and others just look like regular oval/smooth leaves.

Sassafras has been used for hundreds of years by the Native Indians as well as the early settlers to make tea, root beer, medicines, and many other things. It fell out of use, however, because the FDA linked a chemical that is found in it with the possibility of cancer. That didn't stop Aeriel and I from following in the footsteps of our ancestors and making tea out of it anyway! It was really good!

We hiked a total of about 14 miles today through pretty easy terrain. We never strayed too far from Skyline

Drive. Skyline Drive is the best and worst thing about Shenandoah. It's nice because it creates a lot of beautiful vistas, but at the same time I think I would rather be completely removed from all civilization. We walked by a full-blown resort and restaurant today called "Skyland Resort" and are camping tonight near another lodge. All these amenities bring in many tourists who can get quite bothersome for people seeking a more serene experience. It's good and it's bad.

We ended today at Big Meadows Campground - another beautiful spot. I love it out here and am in no way ready to go home yet. We have just over 900 miles to go before Springer Mountain. For the first time this trip the miles to go seem so small to me…

Wednesday, August 27th
Day 63

My First Bear Sighting!
-

Today we did over 20 miles... 21.5 to be exact. That's really good for Cameron! I haven't done that much since before the 4-state challenge! He is finally getting his "trail legs" it seems like. He has even been popping fewer and fewer aspirin lately as well, so I think that is a good sign! Even with the high miles, we had time to stop at one of the Waysides to re-supply as well.

"Waysides" are a Shenandoah National Park equivalent to overpriced convenience stores. Still though, we were able to find everything we needed to make it to Waynesboro. Cameron bought a bottle of wine to celebrate Aeriel's birthday tomorrow! The bottle didn't end up making it that long. We drank it later that evening with Ho and Mandy, two girls we met on the summit of High-top Mountain. We are camping with them tonight a little bit away from the shelter. It's a beautiful evening and High-top Mountain is a perfect opportunity to sleep away from the crowds!

Oh yes, I saw my first bear today as well!! I was hiking in front of Aeriel and Cameron when I heard a large limb break and fall from a tree to my right. I looked up and saw a medium sized bear half falling from the tree. He would let go, fall for a little way, and then grab back on to the tree. Bears are notoriously good climbers but, apparently, they are only good at climbing upwards. I am told that when they are ready to make their decent they simply fall a little ways and then catch themselves – repeating the process until they reach the bottom. Seems like an evolutionary defect to me, but who am I to know!!

Eventually he made it down, looked at me for a few seconds, and then walked across the trail and into the woods on the other side. AMAZING!! They do exist!!!

Wednesday, August 28th
Day 64

Another Bear!
-

What a wonderful Appalachian Trail today was! So much happened! Where do I even start?!?! Fog had moved in through the night so that by the time we woke up we were engulfed in a white milky mist all around us. We said our goodbyes to Ho and Mandy and went on down the trail toward the shelter to get water. At the shelter we ran into a bunch of NOBOs as well as Bear Bait and Amazon (two more girls section hiking the Shenandoah's).

About 6 or 7 miles into our day's hike the fog cleared away and our views returned. I was walking along the trail (again, quite a way in front of Aeriel and Cameron) enjoying the day and, as I turned a pretty sharp corner on the trail, I ran directly into a big black bear. I stopped, and he looked up with a start; I could tell that he was just as surprised to see me as I was to see him. It was maybe only 10 or so feet in front of me, I could see the hairs on its back and the details of his eyes. His head was huge, much bigger up close than what you would expect. We both stood there for a moment just looking at each other. He huffed and took off down the mountainside, falling and rolling and tripping more than running. It was a humorous sight. I am told that if you ever need to run away from a bear, head downhill. The weight of their body presses up against their lungs, capping their top speed. Let's be honest, you will still probably be caught, but maybe you'll get lucky.

We had lunch at Ivy Creek Overlook, and before too long I found myself at Loft Mountain Campground. Since I was ahead of Aeriel and Cameron I, once again, decided to stop and check out Loft Mountain Store: a small convenience store located within sight of the trail. It was here that I met a wonderful couple who I got to talking to. They asked me a ton of questions and seemed super interested in my journey and experiences! After learning that I was hiking with my sister and our friend, they invited us to stay with them at their campsite for the evening and to eat dinner with them. It was awesome! Dinner was a super gourmet meal and was FANTASTIC. They even let me help cook! We stayed up pretty late hanging out and talking about life and the trail. It was a ton of fun, and it was really cool to make two new friends. They are from Wisconsin.

The stars tonight are brilliant. Like the city lights below, they shine on into infinity... yet truly infinitely.

These fabricated lights will dwindle in time into an ever-fading history. The stars will shine on forever.

Friday, August 29th
Day 65

Cameron Stays...
-

This morning started off with an amazing omelet made by the amazing couple that let us set up camp with them last night. Aeriel, Cam, and I hung out with them for a while and hit the trail shortly after they left at 11AM. We left fully stocked with a bunch of vegan food that the couple was nice enough to give us. My favorite was the Hemp Hearts, protein packed wonderfulness that I would buy to eat all the time except for how expensive they are.

Our plan for the next few days is to take it easy into Waynesboro. We have a package that has been sent there but we, because of the weekend, won't be able to pick it up until Monday morning. So, we can take our time getting there! We hiked only 6 miles out of camp to a Shelter called Black Rock Hut. We met a couple at the shelter who were from Florida, and I showed them a few magic tricks and even won half a bottle of whiskey on a bet! I know a few good card tricks that pair well with bar bets, Haha. Never make a bet with a magician!

Also, remember how I said that Cameron was only planning to hike with us for a week or two before leaving for his Graduate Program? Well, he decided today that he wanted to drop out of grad school to hike with us the rest of the way. He has no money but he says that he is planning to put all of his expenses on his credit card. I'm not sure how I feel about that. The guy is nice and all, but he whines a lot and kind of annoys me!

He has made quite a few miles already, but for most part he seems miserable. He complains a lot and is always getting upset at the most trivial of things. I really don't think he has the mindset for long distance backpacking. I am pretty sure he is only staying because he likes Aeriel. Sigh.

Part 9

Waynesboro

Saturday, August 30th
Day 66

Waynesboro, VA
-

Today we hiked almost 20 miles out of Shenandoah National Park and into Waynesboro. Most of the day consisted of flat and downhill walking, but we did have one good climb up to Little Calf Mountain. I'm sad to be leaving the Shenandoah but am glad to move on from the Skyline Drive. It will be nice to get into some less populated parts of the trail again.

As far as trail towns are concerned, Waynesboro is one of the larger ones. At a population of just over 20,000 people, it has everything a thru hiker could possibly need. Plenty of pizza places, inns, restaurants, parks, gear, and even showers at the YMCA! The city has also designated an area in their city park where thru-hikers are allowed to camp at for free! How awesome!

Waynesboro is VERY hiker friendly; everyone here seems to love the AT hikers that come by. In fact, at the road into town we found a bunch of flyers that listed the names of "Trail Angels" living in the area who you could call if you needed anything. All this is good because we are going to be here all day tomorrow!

Aeriel and I are thinking of calling some of the trail angels on the list tomorrow to see if we can do any yardwork or anything to make some extra money. We are running low on our savings and could use any opportunity to make some more! All-in-all the expenses of the trip so far have been very low. For food, we have gotten our expenses down to almost $5 a day. Thanks to Dollar General for that! Other than that, the major expenses we have come from town stops, restaurant food, and the occasional hostel or hotel.

The trail really is a cheap place to be. I'm sure that I spend more money everyday at home. Of course it helps that neither of us have any sort of rent/housing payments, or insurance or anything that we need to worry about back in real life.

Sunday, August 31st
Day 67

Work in Waynesboro
-

Today felt successful despite not walking any distance on the AT. We camped in the city park last night which was quite peaceful. It's a large park with wonderful green grass, a gazebo with electricity and chargers, and even comes complete with spots to hang your hammock. It is quiet, dark, and doesn't feel sketchy at all. I feel very welcomed in this town. We relaxed all morning. Aeriel and I started calling people on the Trail Angel list to see if anyone might have any kind of yardwork that we could help with for some extra cash. My basic sales pitch went something like this:

"Hello, my name is Timothy! I am SOBO hiking the Appalachian trail and found your name on the town's Angel list. I am trying to earn a little money to help finish my hike and was wondering if you may have any yard or housework that needs to be done."

The reply I got after only two calls:

"Oh yes! Of course! Stop by anytime! I'm sure I can find something for you to do!"

Aeriel and I both found people and were able to work for most the day! Everyone we met from the list was SUPER nice. The work I ended up doing ranged from picking weeds to cleaning out litter boxes. It was really simple stuff and the Trail Angels paid handsomely for the services. I got the impression that these people were more interested in helping hikers and hearing our stories than getting any real chores done. What wonderful and kind individuals.

On a side note, it appears that we will be in town for another full day at least. Tomorrow, as it turns out, is Labor Day and the post offices will be closed once again! Damn.

We are receiving a care package from our parents with a small resupply and don't want to miss out! I guess we will be here till the post-offices open on Tuesday!

Monday, September 1st
Day 68

Aiding the Homeless
-

Today was interesting. Mostly we just hung around exploring the city and doing a bit more yardwork. Cameron wanted PizzaHut so we stopped by for a pleasant restaurant experience.

By the time we made it back to our city park the sun was beginning to set and we found a lady in her 40's or 50's frantically unloading a car into the grassy area in front of the pavilion. Apparently, the car wasn't hers (borrowed it from a friend) and she was just using it to move her things from her foreclosed house. She figured that, since they let hikers stay there, it would be okay for her to stay there as well. She had a lot of stuff... A TV, bedding, about a dozen or so trash bags filled with who knows what, lamps, and dozens of other odds and ends that she was stacking under the pavilion.

I don't know what the towns stance is on long-term use of the park by residents is but if their "CAMPING FOR HIKERS ONLY" sign suggested anything to me, it would be that she wouldn't be as warmly welcomed as we have been. She also seemed a bit crazy. Still though, what were we to do? We made small talk and helped her unload a few of the heavier items from her friend's car.

Its not every day you get to help homeless people move into city parks! So that was fun!

Tuesday, September 2nd
Day 69

Back on the Trail Again!!

Today we finally made it out of Waynesboro! The post office opened at 9AM and we were finally able to pick up the box that mom had sent us! In it was all sorts of wonderful goodies for our resupply. There was some beef jerky, Poptarts, instant mashed potatoes, candy, and much more. Thanks mom! The homeless lady we helped move into the park last night was still there when we left, so I have no idea how that situation played out. I kind of want to stick around for another day to see how the townspeople deal with it. Does that make me a bad person? Haha.

We got the chance to chat with both mom and dad on the phone. It was great hearing from them and great to get the care package. When we were finally packed up and ready to go, we said goodbye to Waynesboro and got a hitch back out to the trail. I think I speak for everyone when I say that it felt good to get back walking again after so long a town stop!

We weren't on the trail long before we started running into more SOBO hikers! I met this one guy named

Brad who was Hitchhiking across the country. According to him, he turned 18, and the next day he left everything behind and was on the road hitching rides. It was just a normal day for him when he ran into the Appalachian trail and was fascinated by the idea of walking across the country. So now here he is, walking with us along the trail! It was really cool to talk to him and hear his stories about where he has been and the situations he has gotten himself into. A nice guy. I got his phone number and Facebook info to keep up with his travels.

    I breathe easier in the woods, especially after being in town so long. The simplicity, the smells, and the soft forest sounds are so much more peaceful. We have met a few hikers who seem to hate every aspect of the hike except for the towns. They get into as many towns as they can, as often as they can, and treat the walking in the woods as a necessary evil required in order to continue on with their partying and vacation. I don't understand that mentality at all. Those people should be on a road-trip instead of a walk. Hike your own hike though, my friends.

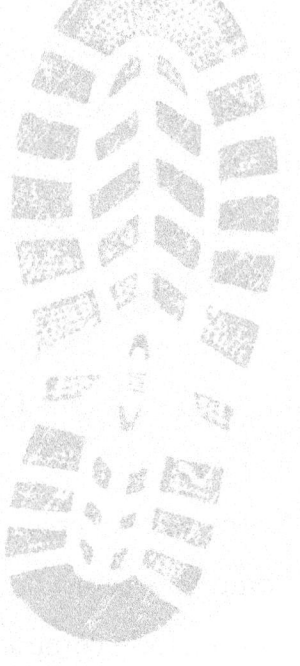

Part 10

Virginia Blues

Wednesday, September 3rd
Day 70

The "Green Tunnel"

It definitely feels good to be back on the trail! I do, however, understand why some people grow weary in Virginia. Miles and miles of rhododendron make the forest floor seem more like an Asian jungle. Rhododendron is an interesting woody shrub, of sorts, with long green leaves and thick clusters of branches. The plant can grow quite tall and easily surrounds entire portions of the trail.

This "green tunnel" can pull a number on your brain, and I often find myself thinking back to all the situations in my life that I am not proud of; there is nothing like backpacking through miles of thick greenery to bring out the self-reflection. It is for this reason I think so many people fail at their thru-hike attempts. It's not the distance. It's not the separation. It's not the physical requirements. It is that it demands something of yourself that most are simply not ready to give: acceptance.

If you cannot come to enjoy your own company and if you cannot come to accept yourself, then I believe that you will never successfully complete a thru-hike.

Hiking through the "green tunnel" can get monotonous, but it is beautiful in its own way as well. There is much more to this area than initially meets the eye. Its not all Rhododendron. There are animals here amongst the plants. Squirrels, chipmunks, birds, and bees run this way and that going about their business. The trees that grow way above the Rhododendron makes the "tunnel" seem much more like a transparent cave. The wind shuffles through the leaves and tickles my senses. There is life all around me and I am only a small part of it.

I am glad I have Aeriel out here with me. While the idea of being completely alone in the woods relying on myself is an amazing one, I do not think I would be enjoying this experience near as much without her. I do believe I would be lonely.

Thursday, September 4th
Day 71

The Priest
-

The Priest is a monster of a Mountain. At 3,100 feet of elevation in 4 miles it is the most continuous up we have had in a long time. I don't think we have had a climb quite like it since Katahdin! It was brutal. While climbing it I realized they call it The Priest because the amount of cursing one does when attempting to summit it requires immediate penance. There is even a logbook at its summit dedicated for this very purpose. All sorts of humorous "Forgive me Father for I have sinned…" type entries.

About two-thirds of the way up the mountain there is this beautiful overlook with the most amazing view. We stopped and rested there for quite some time. The outlook was quite a wonderful break from the "green tunnel" monotony. We could see mountains and trees, valleys and sky. Maybe that's the real reason they call this mountain The Priest: because it is the connection point between us and God.

We've ran into a bunch of college groups today as well. Inevitably I am always the youngest in any group we find ourselves in. I don't mind it though! We are sitting at our campsite tonight with some of these college groups. They really don't seem so much different than me. I find myself wondering what I will be like at their age. I can't imagine that I will have changed that much.

Friday, September 5th
Day 72

Oh, the People you Meet
-

For a while there I thought this would be the first night alone on the trail for me. Ol' Cameron did NOT do well today. His attitude is not well calibrated for long distance backpacking, and he often seems to struggle with his bi-polar mood swings. Anyway, I was waiting for Aeriel and Cam for a long time at the shelter, but they did finally show up. I want to experience camping by myself at some point. It is the one thing I feel as if most thru-hikers experience quite a lot of that I have not yet experienced. I think if I was alone for a long time that I'd get lonely, but I would still like to see what it is like.

This morning we got our earliest start since Cam has been on board: 7:30AM. We walked a total of about 18 miles over decent little ups and downs but nothing too serious. The "green tunnel" was broken by the occasional glorious view. Each time I stop to take in a sight I am still shocked at the beauty around me. It is something that I have not grown tired of out here and something that I don't think I ever will get used too.

I ran into a really weird old guy today as well. Again, I was quite a bit ahead of Aeriel and Cameron (that is becoming somewhat normal) when I walked up to this frail looking man with a long white scraggly beard. We chatted for a bit before he told me that he was excellent at reading peoples features and that he "read my features". He proceeded to tell me that I was, "like…. strange…" That is an exact quote. Gee, thanks old man! Haha! I'm not saying that I'm not strange, but I'm pretty sure he was high.

Oh, the people you meet.

Sunday, September 7th
Day 74

A Wonderful Tradition

Hitch-hiking is always an exciting adventure! It offers a wonderful opportunity to meet new people and share your story. Most people get really sketched-out when they think about riding in a stranger's car, but for AT thru-hikers it is a necessary activity.

Today I have walked about two miles so far to the road into Glasgow. Glasgow is about 6 miles off the trail, so getting a ride is a must. It is either that or spend an entire day road-walking off trail. Normally I would stand by the road and stick out my thumb, but at this place I did not have to. Instead, I got to talking to a man at the parking lot who was loading up his trailer after a camping trip with his family. He was tremendous and offered me a ride into town. It is amazing what can happen through a simple conversation!

Aeriel and Cameron were behind me someplace, and we had agreed to meet in town, so I sat alone in the back of his trailer. Watching the mountains I have been walking through for the past few months fly by at speeds that seemed to me like hundreds of miles an hour seemed odd. Why do we walk when we can drive? I am not sure the exact answer to that question, but the rapidly filling pages of this journal may hold a clue to the answer. The wind blew through my hair and the sun shone on my face. It was a transcendent experience.

I waited in town for a little while for Aeriel and Cam to get their own hitch and meet back up with me. Once they arrived we resupplied at the Dollar Tree (Not as good as Dollar General). We have gotten used to resupplying at Dollar Stores because of how much cheaper they are. We grabbed some pizza at a local place and then got a cramped hitch back out of town. All three of us and our packs had to fit in the back row of a tiny sedan. I'm not sure how we did it, but we did!

Once back on the trail we hiked 9 miles up a tough incline to Marble Spring Campsite for the evening. After building a fire and settling in we presented our town gifts to each other. "Town gifts" is a tradition we came up with where, in each town we stop at, we buy each other small gifts which usually take the form of food and candy that we would not usually carry because of their weight. I think this is a wonderful tradition!

Monday, September 8th
Day 75

Visceral
-

I woke up this morning to a sharp chill in the air. The temperature is getting cooler, and I can feel fall on the air. This makes me very happy! Fall is my favorite season, and I am super excited to experience this annual shift of nature firsthand. Normally I would be spending most of my time inside, either at school or at home. Now, though, I am almost exclusively spending my time outside. I wonder how different the cycles of nature will feel to me? Everything out here is cyclical, and I am a part of that cycle now and have a unique opportunity to feel it on a more visceral level.

Because of the rainy overcast sky and chill of the morning, none of us were in too much of a hurry to get out of bed. A late start it is. Our plan for the day was to eat lunch at Thunder Hill Shelter, a location almost to the top of Apple Orchard Mountain. Being a 7-mile trek almost completely uphill, I started out and left Aeriel and Cameron behind. I find that moving my own pace up difficult sections of the trail is very helpful for my mentality.

The walk up was tough, but gorgeous. Huge boulders spotted the mountainous landscape and I passed one formation called "The Guillotine". The Guillotine is a large boulder wedged between two even larger boulders that you must walk under. I suppose the fear is that it may eventually collapse and that the unlucky hiker stuck below would share a similar fate to the French aristocrats. Well, let them eat cake!

I didn't have to wait for Aeriel and Cameron for too long at the shelter and, because of our late start, we decided to eat lunch there. The rest of the day we spent walking together and discussing fun book ideas based on the AT: post-apocalyptic societies based upon foot travel in the mountain, stories of travelers who fight to overcome and conquer evils (the mountains we summit), and other such ideas – some much more realistic than others. We only hiked 5 more miles for the day to Cornelius Creek Shelter where we made another fire, played solitaire, and fought like animals over Sweetarts: another visceral experience.

Wednesday, September 10th
Day 77

Comradery
-

I couldn't write yesterday because I had thought I lost my pen. It was only after Aeriel lent me this one a few minutes ago that I found my original right where it was supposed to be... strange. Maybe the AT gods are conspiring against me.

Anyway, I digress. Yesterday was another late start of a day but we still managed to hike 18 miles by 5 o'clock over and down some pretty tough terrain. We met 3 SOBOs at the shelter we stayed at: Padre, Lonestar, and Fiver. All three seemed like nice and interesting individuals. I look forward to getting to know them better and seeing them along the trail! They are going at about our pace. Lonestar is from Texas as well (thus his trail name)! Padre offered to walk the section of the trail I missed because of school with me. All I need to do is call him once I get up there! Awesome!

Today was another 18+ mile day, but over easier terrain (mostly just meaningless ups and downs). We ended at Troutville and, because Aeriel needed to stop at the

MedClinic and because Ol' CamCam didn't have a good day, we ended up staying the night at a hotel with LoneStar and the rest of the SOBOs we met. I hung out with them at the 3 Little Pigs BBQ where I told everyone of my pulled pork mishaps in the 100-mile wilderness. We had a great time! After that I met up with Cameron at the pizza hut. He seems to have a special love for Pizza Hut. The rest of the night everyone chilled and hung out together in Lonestar's room.

The comradery among thru hikers, earned through mutual experiences, is difficult to explain. Random people you have never met before feel like best friends you have known forever. It doesn't matter where you come from, what your life back home is like, how old or how young you are, or anything else; you are out there doing the miles like everyone else and, with that, comes the almost automatic respect of your peers. It was an awesome day!

Thursday, September 11th
Day 78

Not much to Report
-

Again, another late start today! It's just so difficult to leave a hotel bed. We got out of Troutville around noon and were able to hike about 16 miles to stay at Campbell Shelter where Fiver and LoneStar joined us. The walk was beautiful! There was a section where we were hiking along some cliffs and were able to see McAfee Knob in the distance. McAfee Knob is famous on the trail for its amazing views and cliffs that overhang nothing. Really! I can't wait to see it tomorrow. Our plan is to wake up super early to make it up there for the sunrise – I hope it works out!

All in all, not much to report for today!

Friday, September 12th
Day 79

Roaring Seas of Grey

Well, our wonderful idea for a sunrise hike didn't really work out. We woke up this morning to a dense fog and general sogginess. By the time we made it up to McAfee Knob nothing had changed. I saw the famous cliffs, but not the famous view. Their edge only slipped away into a roaring sea of grey nothingness. It was beautiful in its own sort of way.

The fog and overcast was not good for the Knob, but it was quite amazing during our approach to "The Dragon Tooth". The Dragon Tooth is a natural stone monolith towering atop a mountain; its shape and size inspiring its name. As we approached the monolith the fog swirled and dashed around it. This created the most mysterious and haunted effect. Truly a sight to behold and one that I feel will remain in my mind for quite some time. I felt the scene on a deeper, more human, level. Much like I was the first to be discovering the place.

Saturday, September 13th
Day 80

Liquid, or Solid?
-

Quick question: is a giraffe a liquid or a solid? Well, an argument could be argued for either, or both. A giraffe is held together by a solid exterior, yet, like most mammals, it is made up of a majority water. A fun and stupid question to ponder while on a walk in the woods, right? Well, Cameron didn't think so. Today was another long day filled with rain and fog. To fight off the monotony, Aeriel, Cam, and I decided to play 20 Questions. Well, it was Aeriel's turn to think of something and when Cameron asked if it was a solid or a liquid all hell broke loose. Aeriel answered: "It's both!"

Maybe this wasn't the best or most accurate response to the question, but ol' Cameron took it very seriously and then proceeded to freak out when learning that the answer was in reference to a giraffe. And I mean literally freaked out, like he lost it for a bit. I am not sure if he is a sociopath or if he just can't handle certain things, but I do not think this guy is built for the unique stresses of the trail.

Don't get me wrong. I don't actually think that Cameron is a sociopath, he is mostly nice. It's not like he is going to snap one day and murder us in our sleep, but I wouldn't be surprised if he just sat down in the middle of the trail and refused to move like a small child throwing a tantrum. Both Aeriel and I are beginning to think that his decision to quit grad school may have been a bad one.

The fog and rain never let up throughout the day, and we made it a whole 18-20 miles without so much as a view. It's sad because I feel like this area of rolling hills and farmland would be beautiful. We are camping tonight next to the 2nd oldest oak tree on the AT. It is a massive thing about 18 feet around and tucked away on the edge of a pasture. It's quite marvelous to think of the history and stories it has seen and been a part of during its over 300-year life.

Aeriel and Cameron set up their tent under my hammock and tarp as an attempt to stay dry. Aeriel's tent is apparently starting to spring some leaks.

Monday, September 15th
Day 82

Heaven on Earth
-

    I missed another day of writing yesterday. Not because of disappearing and reappearing pens like last time, but because I lost my light somewhere along the way and couldn't see in the dark last night. I will have to get a new one in the next town! Light in the dark is another thing people take for granted in "real" life. Out here the only thing we have to illuminate the pitch black at night are our flashlights and headlamps. Without them, it is almost impossible to see. Especially when under a thick canopy of trees and brush.

    We walked 18 miles yesterday starting out at the huge oak tree and ending at Bailey Gap Shelter. We ended up being the only ones at the shelter and had to spend the night there on our own. The weather cleared up and the day ended up being a nice one with only a few major ups and downs.

    Today was BEAUTIFUL. Rice Field Shelter (which we only walked past), is stunning. Set on the edge of a large field, it overlooks what I believe to be the most magnificent and marvelously pleasing valley I have ever set my eyes on. Stretched out in front of me were miles of fields, farms, and trees nestled between impressive mountains. The glistening sun perfected this postcard scene. I am pretty sure I have discovered heaven on earth. Who knew it was in Virginia all this time?

We were planning on another 18-mile day today but, because of a re-route on the trail, ended up going 23.7 all the way to Pearisburg. We got a hitch in, re-supplied, and got a hitch back out to our camp. In town we discovered a Chinese restaurant that has a $5 All-You-Can-Eat special going on tomorrow. We are thinking that another round of hitches back to town in the morning may be a worthwhile endeavor!

Tuesday, September 16th
Day 83

A $5 Buffet

When stopping to think about it, a $5 All-You-Can-Eat buffet may not be the smartest place to go. I mean, what does that say about the food? How are they even making money? Are they buying quality ingredients? These questions and more I ignored while chowing down on all manner of mystery meats.

Pearisburg is a great place, and its Chinese buffet was even better. We got another hitch into town this morning specifically to visit this restaurant that had the $5 buffet special going on. Well, we certainly got our money's worth. By the time we were done eating none of us could move. We crashed on a little patch of grass outside the restaurant and just laid there digesting for a good 2 or 3 hours. Calorie deficiency defeated.

When we did finally make it back to the trail it was already well past noon, and we had miles to walk. We started up a mountain toward a place called "Angels Rest". For a place with such a wonderful name, the climb was hell on earth. Laden with full packs from our resupply and still stuffed with cheap Chinese food, we struggled up endless switch backs.

The only redeeming quality was the mountain itself. The trees were old and massive, and there was very little underbrush, only a carpet of leafy plants that grew maybe a foot or two off the ground. It was like walking through a cathedral of green with massive brown pillars extending indefinitely upwards to support a ceiling of sky. And there I was: walking through it and suffering from too much cheap Chinese food.

Angels Rest was wonderful, a perfect place to stop and rest with amazing views of the nearby countryside. The rest of the day was much nicer as well. Some down, a little more up, but mostly flat. We made it to Docs Knob Shelter, about 8 miles from the road, and decided to stop for the day. Having a bit of time to kill, Aeriel and I taught Cameron how to play Canasta. Canasta is a card game that Aeriel and I grew up playing with my grandmother. It can be played with 2 – 4 people. Cameron is sort of terrible at it, but he did just learn it!

Wednesday, September 17th
Day 84

We Found the Missing Link
-

Today everyone was feeling much better. I can't speak for the others, but I had a few interesting bowel movements in the night thanks to the Chinese food. We hiked a total of 15 miles over all flat and downhill terrain. It was a pretty nice day altogether, but we really had no views and were basically walking through the "green tunnel" yet again. Still though, the forest is beautiful, and being surrounded by it is an experience in-and-of itself. About halfway through the day's walk we ran into Lonestar and Fiver again. It's always good to see and catch up with fellow hikers! Everyone is hiking the same trail, but the difference in stories, experiences, and what everyone noticed differently is very interesting.

We ended our hike at a place called Dismal Falls. It was a beautiful area where the water cascaded down layers of rock. It didn't seem like a dismal place to me! It seems like the perfect swimming place! I was able to wash my feet and legs, it felt wonderful. Our Campsite was just a short walk from the falls, and I can hear the water rushing and tumbling from my hammock. It is very relaxing.

As the sun began to set we met two more female SOBO hikers out for a large section. Their trail names were Miss, and Link. Together they liked to be referred to as "MissNLink" or "MissingLink" like the evolutionary step between monkeys and man. This may give you an idea of their personalities. It appears that the proof for Darwin's theory isn't found in the fossil records at all, but hiking along on the AT! They are very fun and nice people! I am sure we will be seeing them down the trail again as well.

Thursday, September 18th
Day 85

Sub Sandwiches!
-

We had inspiration to make our miles today! Aunt S and Uncle G planned to meet us at US52, the road into Bastian Va. We knew that if they were coming to meet us that it meant lots of food, a hotel, and a day of relaxation and rest! And we were not disappointed. The 18 mile walk to the road was uneventful. A few ups and downs but nothing major. We were walking through forests of rhododendron the entire time.

I was ahead of Aeriel and CamCam when I made it to the road, and Auntie S and Uncle G met me there with the most amazing and wonderful sub sandwiches that I could possibly have imagined. Auntie S and Uncle G are quite possibly the greatest people and most amazing trail angels of all time! I didn't wait for Aeriel and Cameron to join us to dig in!

We stayed at a hotel that night a short ways off the trail. We were able to get showers, do laundry, and relax. It was really nice! It is always so shocking to me to see just how dirty I get out here. I'm sure that I constantly smell horrible! It makes me wonder if this is how people lived for their entire lives back in the dark ages. I'm sure that people who lived in the country back then had their fair share of swims in the river, but did they use soap? What about the people in the cities? If I am any sort of indicator, it must have smelt awful.

Friday, September 19th
Day 86

Nothing Much at All
-

Today was a day that consisted of doing nothing much at all! Which was wonderful! We relaxed in the hotel room, read, resupplied at Walmart, got food at Wendy's for Lunch, got food at a Mexican place called El Patio for dinner, and all around had a great relaxing time hanging out with my aunt and uncle. The Mexican food was especially great!

Saturday, September 20th
Day 87

Another Easy Day!
-

Despite all the great things about being in town, I always enjoy my first few steps back into the woods. Being back in the woods is like breathing that sigh of relief once you finally get in bed after a long, hard day. Auntie S and Uncle G dropped us off back at the trail around 10:30AM. We said out goodbyes and our thank yous, and our I love yous, and then we were on our way.

We walked only about 12 miles over pretty nice terrain to the next shelter which was called Jenkins Shelter. We decided to stay there for the evening and were able to get in a few games of Canasta in before Miss and Link showed up! Cameron is still terrible at Canasta, and I found myself taking it easy on him despite myself.

We spent the rest of the evening talking, hanging out, and playing card games. Miss taught us a new game called 3-13. It was fun and a lot like a rummy game.

Sunday, September 21st
Day 88

Chestnut Knob
-

I do not know the history of Chestnut Knob Shelter, but I am sure it's a fascinating one! Chestnut Knob Shelter is a fully enclosed stone building standing alone in a field atop a mountain. It seems like it may have been someone's house back in the day! It is a unique shelter on the trail and certainly is one of my favorites so far! Inside there are wooden bunks, a picnic table, and a fireplace. Unfortunately, somewhere along the way, someone thought it would be a good idea to cement up the fireplace. Very unfortunate! I'm not sure why they felt the need to do that.

When we woke up this morning, we could tell that it would be another foggy and rainy day. The sky was dark and grey, and the wind had been picking up in the night. The pressure in the air seemed funny, too. I have found that I have become more in tune to atmospheric pressure. Sure enough, we ended up doing plenty of walking in the fog, mist, and rain. All in all, it was not so bad though! Some people are miserable in the rain and wet, but I find that I do alright in it. It simply is what it is! Yes, the wet makes me feel sticky and uncomfortable, but I find it helpful to focus on the trees and nature. We walked through a beautiful grove of wild apple trees.

We did a lot of field walking, and it was pretty with the fog and mist. After a while, though, the rain got harder and more intense. I did end up becoming fairly miserable despite my best efforts.

By the time we made it to Chestnut we were all soaked through. We have had our fair share of rain but walking through miles of open and exposed fields in the onslaught was something special. I think I need to upgrade my raingear. After drying off in the shelter for a few hours for lunch we decided to just stay put instead of fighting the rain again. Miss, Link, and two women in their 60's ended up staying with us in the shelter. It makes me happy that older people are out here enjoying the trail as well, It gives me hope that I may still be backpacking when I am their age!

I am glad we have a fully enclosed house for tonight!

Monday, September 22nd
Day 89

Experiencing
-

    During the night I could tell that the rain was subsiding somewhat and by the time we packed up in the morning it stopped completely. Unfortunately, the rain had only been replaced by thick fog and a fine and consistent mist. In a way this mist is worse than the rain. It doesn't bombard you, but it permeates everything. I felt as if I was walking on a mountain in a fishbowl. Everything stuck to me, my pack was soaked, my rain poncho was soaked, and after only a few miles my fingers were in a continuous state of raisining.

    We did have some reprieve from the mist and fog as the day went on. It cleared up a bit and the sun poked out through the blanket of clouds. The temperature shifted as well. A cold front was coming through. Honestly, it was quite refreshing! We hiked about 18 miles through forests without much in the way of views. Overall, it was a normal and uneventful day! I really don't have too much to write about!

When I get into conversations with people about my experiences thus far on the trail, they almost inevitably ask about what I do all day. Mostly, as it turns out, I just walk. It's sometimes difficult for me to romanticize it, or to explain just what it is like. I walk, I eat, I sleep, and I do my best to write. I sometimes meet interesting people, and I occasionally find myself in interesting situations. But for the most part, I walk.

Explained in that way, long distance backpacking doesn't sound like much fun, and I imagine that for some it would be hell on earth (Cameron?). Really though, there is something much more to it that I find very difficult to explain. Either you get it, or you don't. And the people who have never set out to walk across the country through the mountains won't possibly understand until they do. It doesn't sound like fun, and days like today sound outright miserable. It's not, though. Its enlightening. Its freedom. It's experiencing in its purest form.

We are camping away from a shelter tonight on top of Little Bushy Mountain. I like Little Bushy Mountain.

Tuesday, September 23rd
Day 90

A 50-Mile Day?

Last night on top of Little Bushy Mountain got RREEEAAALLLYYY cold! I wish I had a thermometer to measure it! I can't wait for winter to come; I am excited for it. I have always liked cooler and cold weather, and I have found that I am no different out here!

Today we hiked only a handful of miles to Atkins, VA. The trail passes right through this little town along Interstate 81. As far as a town goes, it isn't much, just a few buildings, a gas station, a Dollar General, and "The Barn Restaurant". Really though, that's all that a thru-hiker needs! I am currently sitting at The Barn Restaurant waiting for my ordered hamburger. I am super excited for that!!

Aeriel and I are discussing the prospects of a potential 50-mile day. We both are interested in attempting one, but ol' Cameron doesn't seem so keen on the idea. We are thinking about possibly sending Cameron ahead to Damascus, VA from Troutdale with our packs. Damascus is almost exactly 50 miles from Troutdale, so it would be the perfect stretch for such an attempt! And if Cameron shuttled ahead with our packs, I have no doubt that we would be able to pull it off! We haven't decided for sure if we are going to do it or not, but we are considering it!

Wednesday, September 24th
Day 91

A Snapshot of the Past
-

The Partnership Shelter is a wonderful place. The shelter itself sits right near highway 16 and a visitor center. It's made of logs, has two stories, and comes complete with a shower! Not too many AT shelters can boast such a claim. There is even a nearby pizza place that will deliver to the location. Another one of those few "god shelters" we have run across.

Our walk today was nice. We had a few ups and downs, but the forest has been beautiful. Around lunch time we came across an old one room schoolhouse that was in operation from the late 1890's until 1937. It was built in the same location as two previous schoolhouses that had burnt down. It is now preserved as a sort of museum; it is open to the public and everything has been kept as it would have been. It was like walking through a snapshot of a wonderfully simple time. I find myself thinking of what it must have been like to live in this area as a child walking to a tiny single-room school every day. A far cry from the massive public schools we have in many cities and towns today. It's hard to fathom exactly how far our society has come in less than one-hundred years. I wonder if we have really changed so much. My guess is that we haven't, we only like to think we have because our technology seems so revolutionary. We are still creatures with an ancient biology and remembering that may be more important for our future than we think. Who knows?

So, today we walked less than 10 miles, got to take a shower, relax, and spend time with fellow hikers! Miss and Link are camping here with us and insisted on ordering pizza! Of course, I didn't adamantly object to that proposal.

Part 11
A 50 Mile Day

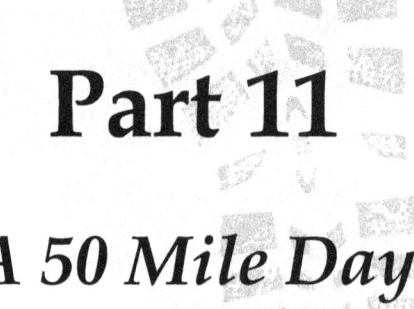

Thursday, September 25th
Day 92

Preparing
-

Today Aeriel and I decided that we definitely want to attempt the 50-mile day. We have had a few slow restful days now and we want to see if we can do it! Our plan is to stay in Troutdale tonight, and then leave early next morning for the 50 miles into Damascus. Cameron will get a shuttle and take our packs and himself up to Damascus to meet us. Although we are slackpacking, we are still walking 50 miles over tough Virginia mountains in less than 24 hours. Not having our packs will enable us to walk faster for longer but, at the same time, we won't be able to make camp if we need too. We won't have our sleeping bags, and we won't have any safety nets. To complete our self-imposed challenge, we are removing the very things that could possibly save us if something goes wrong. A potentially dangerous proposition.

Today we walked 14 miles into Troutdale. We had pretty flat walking (only small hills) for most of the day, but right at the end we had a pretty tough uphill climb. We are staying at "Troutdale Church Hostel"; a wonderful place that provides a bunkhouse, showers, tenting, and even allows you to attend church in hiker attire. If it was Sunday, I would have attended! Such a wonderful and nice place.

Miss and Link managed to keep up with us today as well and, once we all got settled in, they insisted on trying to put my hair up in a ponytail. I don't think it looks so bad! I haven't had a haircut now for a few months and my hair is certainly getting long.

Tomorrow we will be attempting our 50-mile day. We will have to average an over 2 mph walking speed all day long with no breaks. Realistically we are hoping to walk much faster than that. We are hoping that without full packs this will be easily doable. Aeriel has a small day pack that we will be bringing to carry food, our jackets, headlamps, and our first aid kit (complete with an emergency blanket). Other than these small comforts, which we will be taking turns carrying, we will be alone.

Friday, September 26th
Day 93

The 50-Mile Day
-

50 miles.... That's FIVE-ZERO miles. That's five ten-mile days stacked on top of each other. That's practically two back-to-back marathons. On top of the distance, we have some tough climbs as well. Southern Virginia, as it turns out, it quite mountainous!

We said goodbye to Cameron, our backpacks and to Miss and Link around 10AM this morning. The only things we took with us were Aeriel's day-pack, a few water bottles, some snacks, and our flashlights. If something happened, we wouldn't have our shelters, extra clothes, or much of anything at all. We are on our own! Slackpacking is amazing, but it does come at the expense of some added risk – especially at such large distances. We could always find a road crossing and hitch hike out if we absolutely needed to; in our minds, however, it was do or die!

The morning started out wonderfully, in fact, the whole first 25 miles were quite nice. The day was beautiful; the sun was shining through the woods and Aeriel and I, free of the weight of our packs, were practically running down the trail. We both felt amazing and climbed up Pine Mountain and up into the Grayson Highlands and to Thomas Knob Shelter like it was nothing. We passed a lot of interesting ruins from people who used to live in the area. The most notable of was "The Scales Livestock Corral": a large fenced in circular area that they used to use to herd up and weigh cattle before their march to the big cities. The cattle was sold by the pound, so weighing them in before the long trek was only a sort of financial backhandery. Haha. I wonder how much weight I have lost?

The Grayson Highlands were beautiful as well. At around mile 15 of our day, we crossed into the State Park and were quickly greeted by the panoramic views and the stunning fields of grass that the area is known for. There are wild ponies that roam the area as well and are known for trying to steal hiker's food whenever possible. We even heard a story of a hiker who lost their entire food bag to one and was forced to turn back to the nearest town to re-re supply.

We left The Grayson Highlands as the sun was setting. Its evening glow produced the most beautiful golden rays that paired wonderfully with the rolling hills and grassy meadows of the area. A spot I would like to come back too!

With the darkness came its normal level of monotony, tiredness, and mental fatigue. But we still had lots of miles to walk! Between 10pm and Midnight we walked by this camp (it had bathrooms) filled with loud and rowdy people. It seemed pretty sketchy! The night went on though, and we kept walking. At around 2AM the trail led us to a field with lots of cow patties. Somehow, we lost the trail and ended up walking aimlessly in this cow field for about 20 – 30 minutes searching for it again. Sometimes walking in the dark can be problematic!

The rest of the night went by without too much to say. It was dark, and we walked. The last 10 miles of our hike felt like they would never end. At that point we were basically zombies! We made it into Damascus around 8AM and met up with Cameron at a place called "Hiker's Inn" where we promptly crashed. We finished two hours early! Overall, an awesome experience! I am glad we did it.

Saturday, September 27th
Day 94

Damascus
-

I spent today sleeping. We got into town from our 50-mile day early in the morning and promptly went to sleep. I woke up again around 1PM and decided to explore town and resupply. Damascus is an awesome hiker paradise. There are tons of outfitters, outdoorsy adventure companies, and hostels. It's also really pretty! I walked to the Food City for my resupply and, since I was still tired, bought a Rock Star energy drink. This was the first energy drink I have ever had, and it did a wonderous job of waking me up!

Aeriel discovered that there was a movie being played at the local library so, around 4PM, we stopped by to watch it with the local townspeople. They were showing "Divergent": a movie based on a series of novels by Veronica Roth. The movie was simply alright, but it was a fun experience! After our movie we went to Blue Blaze Café for dinner and to watch the A&M football game for Cameron. Cameron is very into college football and does his best to watch as many games as possible. I am not a huge college football fan, but I do enjoy watching the games. A cute girl smiled at me at the bar!

We are spending the night in Damascus again tonight, but we plan to get an early start tomorrow!

Part 12

Goodbye Virginia, Hello Tennessee!

Sunday, September 28th
Day 95

Goodbye Virginia Blues

Today we crossed into Tennessee!! Woohoo! Virginia is finished and done with! We have been in Virginia now for over 500 miles, just about a quarter of the entire trail, and getting to the end of it is a huge milestone! Statistically, the majority of NOBO hikers who make it through the first two-weeks quit in Virginia. Good-bye Virginia Blues! I'm really looking forward to Tennessee and North Carolina; the Smoky Mountains in particular! I can't wait!

We have just under 450 miles left to go on our walk. I am starting to see the end in my mind. I believe that I am mostly sad at the proposition of finishing... Obviously I have always known that the trail will end, but it's really just now hitting me. I am most certainly not ready to get off yet! We are camping tonight at Iron Mountain Shelter, about 20 or so miles for the day. We must average around 16 – 18 miles a day from here in order to make it to Springer Mountain by the 25th of October. I think mom, dad, and Slater (my brother) will be coming out to meet us and walk with us at the end!

Monday, September 29th
Day 96

McGangbang
-

It is crazy what I would do for some McDonalds. It's gooey, fatty, calorie dense wonderfulness is more valuable to me than gold out here (gold is heavy, I do NOT want to carry that). We made it about 16 miles today and are camping in the "Shook Branch Recreation Area" next to a wonderful lake. The lake is beautiful enough, but the real reason we decided to stop at this spot is because it is right next to US Highway 321.

US Highway 321 is quite a special highway, not because it's that great of a highway, but because 3 miles down it there happens to be a McDonalds. Aeriel, Cameron, and I have recently been discussing a few of the better menu options at McDonalds. First, we have my personal favorite: The Triple Double. The Triple Double is made by ordering three double cheeseburgers and stacking them on top of each other to create a tower of six patties. Another pretty good option that Cameron informed me of is the "McGangbang". The McGangbang is created by placing a spicy chicken between two cheeseburgers (or two double cheeseburgers if you want the Deluxe McGangbang). As it turns out, there are all kinds of ways to make the Dollar Menu at McDonalds more hiker friendly.

Anyway, Aeriel and I got a pretty sketchy hitch into town with a guy who was probably high. He was nice enough and told us how he just got off work, but the fact that I could see the ground through the floor of his car did not inspire too much confidence in the quality of his employment. But, despite the quality of the car, we made it to McDonalds safely and were able to fill up on the wonderfulness that it is. We got a hitch back out to the lake and our campsite without a problem, even though it was dark!

Tuesday, September 30th
Day 97

Cameron the WazWillow
-

So, tomorrow marks 25 days left to go on the trip... I'm almost done! I'm not ready to go back, not yet. Who knows though, maybe by the time October 25th rolls around I will be begging to get off! I doubt it, but we will see! Haha

We hiked 17.9 miles today up and down some decent mountains. We ran into a bunch of volunteers working on trial maintenance and on re-building an old bridge. It was awesome to see how it was all coming together! We got to help them out a bit carrying supplies back and forth. For the most part, the AT is maintained and kept up by an army of volunteers organized into various groups and organizations. It is their hard work and passion that keeps the trail in such good condition! Without these wonderful people, hiking on the Appalachian Trail would most likely be a constant bush whacking experience. So, thank you to them!

Ol' Cameron was not having a very good day today. He was hiking along at a very slow pace for some unknown reason. He was also in an especially pissy mood for reasons that go well above Aeriel's and my head. I have a new term to describe the type of person Cameron is: a "WazWillow". A WazWillow is someone who is always gloomy and downtrodden (much like a Willow Tree). WazWillows don't stop at being gloomy though. They go a step beyond that by pissing on everyone else's good time. Waz – as in taking a waz, or taking a piss or, in this case, pissing on everyone else who is trying to enjoy what happens to be a very good day.

Perhaps I exaggerate a bit too much, we have had all kinds of good times with him, but he certainly does have the tendency to freak out, get depressed, and do crazy things. The trail tests people. It takes you out of your comfort zone and applies unique pressures onto both the mind and the body that very few people will face in the "real life". Some people simply do not have the mental fortitude.

Wednesday, October 1st
Day 98

The WazWillowiest

Out of all the WazWillows in the world, Cameron is the WazWilloweiest.... We walked an easy 16 or 17 miles today over pretty easy terrain: just a bunch of little ups and downs. Despite this, Cameron was lagging. There is absolutely nothing wrong with walking at a slower pace than your traveling companions, but Ol' Cam seems to take it very personally.

It is very common on the trail for people who are in a group to agree on a place to meet at lunchtime or at the end of the day and then walk at different paces to get there. It is also very common for groups of thru-hikers to not see each other much between the agreed upon meeting places. I don't think Cameron likes being the slowest walker though, and I don't think he likes the feeling of being "left behind" even though we were never more than 10-30 minutes ahead of him.

At some point in the afternoon Aeriel and I split off from Cameron to walk more quickly and told him that we would wait for him at the road going into Roan Mountain

Tennessee where our plan was to resupply. Well, we got there and waited for him. We waited, and we waited, and we waited. Eventually we began to get worried. Aeriel decided to run back up the trail to find him (I stayed behind to watch the packs). Well, maybe 10 minutes later, Aeriel returned with a very upset and angry Cameron. He stormed right past me without saying a word and continued up the trail in a hurried state. He was clearly pissed about something and, needless to say, I was confused. Apparently, he had stopped at a much smaller barely paved road .2 miles back thinking that it was road into town. Not finding Aeriel and I waiting for him, he assumed that we had simply deserted him. This small barely paved road could barely be considered a road either. Neither Aeriel or I even considered the possibility that he might mistake it for a main road. I'm sure the feeling of being deserted wasn't a good one, but he didn't have to react so poorly to a simple misunderstanding.

Aeriel and I were very confused about his reaction and ended up getting an easy hitch into town to resupply. Seeming that Ol' Cameron stormed off down the trail, Aeriel and I bought extra food for him (we knew he didn't have any). The hitch in and out were both really beautiful. I saw a super steep horse pasture that was built on the side of a mountain! Tomorrow we are hiking over an area called the Roan Highlands. I'm really excited for this section and am pretty sure it is going to be one of the most memorable parts of the trail!

Aeriel and I found Cameron about 3 miles south on the trail just laying on the ground with his legs propped up on a log. It took everything in me not to freak out at him. I'm still not sure if it's a good thing or a bad thing that I didn't.

We passed the 400 mile marker today as well, not too long to go to the finish!

Thursday, October 2nd
Day 99

Alpine Christmas
-

All my hopes of the Roan Mountain Highlands were shattered today... in the most wonderful way. Today was sooo amazingly beautiful and, despite the almost continuous uphill walking, I enjoyed every moment of it. The weather was perfect for backpacking: cool and windy. As we gained elevation the smells of the pine trees took over in a way that I can only describe as an "Alpine Christmas". The whole area was amazing. The cool fall air was amazing, the "balds" – the treeless mountain tops which the area is known for - were amazing, the trees were amazing, the birds were amazing, everything was amazing! I am truly speechless at the vast beauty that I am surrounded by and can't quite place the feelings of elation and wonder that I feel. It is times like today that I understand the true limitations of my meager vocabulary... I need to work on that.

It appears that around every bend in the trail something new and something spectacular was waiting for us. We saw Overmountain Shelter: a random hay barn condemned by the forest service to die. It has a history stretching back to the revolutionary war when the early Americans used it as a shelter while crossing the mountains to cut off a British attack. it seems a shame to me that no one is working to keep it kept up.

We walked through the fields and glory of Jane and Round Balds – two mountains with panoramic views stretching dozens and dozens of miles. We also got to see Roan High Knob Shelter. At 6,285 feet of elevation, it is the highest shelter on the AT. I really cannot describe everything I saw and felt and sensed in a way that one can understand… some things go beyond words and beyond photos in a way you can only understand if you experience it yourself.

We managed to hike about 20 miles today despite many breaks and many stops (we were able to play two hands of Canasta). Now we are camped in Hughes Gap next to an old gravel road that doesn't seem like it has much traffic.

Friday, October 3rd
Day 100

100 Days in the Wilderness
-

It has now been 100 days in the wilderness for me. 100 days of walking. 100 days of adventure. Simultaneously, it feels like it has been half that time and twice that time. I feel like I have lived more in the last 100 days than I have in the last 5 years. I have seen mountains, I have seen forests, I have met the most amazing people, I have experienced the craziest highs, and I have experienced the lowest of lows. I have truly lived. How many people can say that with true conviction? I would venture to guess not so many.

Today we hiked 25 miles and ended at Curley Maple Gap Shelter about 5 miles from Erwin, TN. Most of the day was spent descending from the heights of Roan Mountain, but we did have a few decent uphill battles. I can tell that Aeriel did not like going so far. I don't blame her – it was tough. It seems like it is going to rain tonight as well, the sky has grayed, and clouds have been rolling in. It is also getting chilly again; I hope we don't get hypothermic!

Saturday, October 4th
Day 101

Sog to the Bones
-

Last night was as cold and as wet as I feared it might be. I was fine in my hammock – high and dry – but this morning was chilly and seemed to sog everyone to the bones. It's possible it may have frozen in the night. The general mood and demeanor of the group seemed equally affected. Aeriel and Cameron's tent seemed to do fine last night as well (they didn't get too wet), but it was clear that some sun would do everyone good. It was for this reason Cameron decided to break out his credit card and purchase a $100 hotel room in Erwin for all of us. I wasn't about to say no, haha. A hotel room sounds quite nice right about now! Maybe having a financially irresponsible WazWillow on board isn't the worst thing in the world.

It has only been about a week since my last shower, but as you may have guessed, a backpacker can build up quite a bit of grime and smell in that time! Ol' Cameron has his negative moments, and I still don't think his mind is built for the unique stresses of backpacking, but he is a decent guy and is quite kind when it comes down to it.

Aeriel and I certainly would not be able to afford a $100 hotel room. Perhaps I am too hard on him.

The reason for the higher expense of the hotel room soon became apparent: there is an apple festival going on!! How awesome is that! Erwin is a smaller town but still a bit bigger than most small towns. It is also well known for its apple festival.

Every year they shut down many of the streets and let local farmers, artisans, shops, and stores set up booths to showcase their work and sell their products. It was a ton of fun!! I love meeting local people and experiencing local cultures and celebrations. Moments like this apple festival are the things that I never expected to experience on the AT but have become one of my favorite aspects of the trip. You never know who you will meet and what kinds of situations you will find yourself in. It is truly a beautiful experience.

Sunday, October 5th
Day 102

On Small Town America
-

Small town America is a strange place. Walking down the deserted streets you wonder how possibly the town scratches up enough money to survive. Further, why does someone spend time making it look pretty if there is no one to see? Perhaps for their own enjoyment? Their own pleasure? How long will it be before small-town America dries up completely and is stomped out of existence by the bigger cites? When the children finally get their wish to leave and the old finally die? Alas! Then what?

Perhaps one of the most unexpected aspects of hiking the Appalachian Trail for me has been the sheer number of small communities and small towns/cities I have had the unique pleasure of visiting. I feel like visiting these places in the way I have is the best way to tour the true beauty of America: the people and the places you have never heard of, the people and the places that exist on their own with their own communities and their own culture. The United States is huge, and there are so many different people and so many different places. I only wish I could spend more time in some.

We left Erwin in the afternoon and hiked the first 6 miles up Big Bald Mountain and ended at No Business Knob Shelter. We gained about 2,000 feet of elevation out of Erwin and got to see some really beautiful views of the town.

Monday, October 6th
Day 103

No Need to Imagine
-

Imagine, for a moment, a field of grass. This grass is blowing gently in the wind and is part of a larger network of fields that extend across multiple mountains and multiple peaks. From these green fields of grass, you can see distant mountains and hills slightly obscured by haze and atmosphere. All around you, in every direction, sights are beheld that you can barely manage to tear your eyes from. To the west you see rays of sunshine filtering through a sea of white cumulous clouds, to the north you see a distant thunderstorm pouring millions of gallons of water onto revitalized ecosystems, and to south and east you see miles and miles of seemingly untouched wilderness of the same.

Now imagine, for just a second, that you do not need to imagine such a place. That this is a place that exists and that this is a place you can experience for yourself. If only you were so inclined. The vast expanses of the world are mind boggling, and I count myself blessed beyond words to have even the small understanding of that expanse that I now possess.

We hiked about 20 miles today over Big Bald and Little Bald Mountains. The views and experience of it was, once again, beyond my ability to string together words. We ended our day at Hogback Ridge Shelter.

Tuesday, October 7th
Day 104

A Challenge for Me!
-

Today I met three wonderful gentlemen at the Flint Mountain Shelter (where we are staying for the night) named Tom, Darren, and David. Tom, Darren, and David are just out on the trail for a few days and are planning to get off the trail after finishing up their hike after a short day tomorrow.

Well, I got to talking to them and they ended up telling me about their plans to drive to Hot Springs, NC for dinner at a restaurant tomorrow after they get back to their car. Well, as it turns out, the Appalachian Trail goes directly into Hot Springs in about 26 miles. Wanting to see if I could actually do it, Tom, Darren and David offered to buy me dinner if I could make that distance and meet them before their 7 o'clock reservation.

Sounds like a challenge for me! Aeriel and Cameron don't want to partake but say that they will meet me in Hot Springs on the following day. I think it should be a fun little challenge!

Wednesday, October 8th
Day 105

Alone
-

Today I did 26 miles by myself. It was awesome. I started my trek at 9:30am with the goal of making it all the way to HotSprings by 7pm at the latest to meet up with Tom, Darren, and David at the Iron Horse Bar. Anything for some free food! Aeriel and Cameron don't plan to join me on the adventure so I will also be camping alone for the first time on this trip. I have been wanting to camp alone on the trail for quite some time now, so I am excited about that!

I started out this morning by hiking up Big Butt Mountain (a wonderful name for a mountain). Big Butt Mountain is full of wonderful views and cliff overlooks. Unfortunately, though, it was pretty foggy so I didn't get the full experience. I also didn't see any big butts around, so that was slightly disappointing. The fog must have hidden them. The sky and rain cleared up as the day progressed and everything became quite nice and beautiful by around lunch time.

I descended Big Butt Mountain, Climbed Spring Mountain and Rich Mountain, and eventually descended the most beautiful trail to Hot Springs. There were almost continuous views from rock outcroppings that overlooked French Broad River and the town of Hot Springs itself.

I made it into town a bit before 6:30pm and managed to meet up with Tom and his group! They seemed surprised that I had actually made it! True to their word, they treated to me to the "Iron Horse Burger"; it was the most amazing hamburger of my life. It was gooey and wonderful and was topped with fried onions, applewood smoked bacon, cheese, tomatoes, lettuce, and perfection. I got onion rings on the side! Restaurant quality food hits a little different after a few weeks of trail food. I am truly appreciative of these quality individuals for inviting me along!

After dinner, I said goodbye to my new friends and made my way back a short distance along the trail to set up camp. I ended up choosing a spot right next to the riverbank and within eyeshot of the trail. I didn't want Aeriel or Cameron to miss me if they happened by! Being next to the river was nice and really relaxing.

Thursday, October 9th
Day 106

HotSprings
-

I woke up this morning still alone. Fine by me! Aeriel and Cameron would soon be along and my lonesome adventure would be at its close. Not having too much to do, and not wanting to miss my fellow wanderers, I relaxed. The sounds of the river which lulled me to a peaceful slumber the night before continued its unabated course. It is becoming ever clearer that fall is taking hold on the world around me. Trees are losing more and more of their leaves and the cool breezes are becoming ever more pervasive. I love it.

Hot Springs is an awesome little town that has been a resort destination since the 1800's. The hot springs in the area are well known for their healing properties and beautiful mountain settings. Even the Native American's who lived in the area knew of them and often held spiritual ceremonies and rituals in the area. I wish we had more time to visit the area and maybe even enjoy some of the hot springs! Too bad we are running on monetary fumes at this point! Haha.

Aeriel and Cameron came along before too long and we were re-united at last! We briefly caught up on each other's adventures from the day before and then headed into town to resupply at the local Dollar General. We only made it 3 or so miles out of town and ended our day at Deer Park Mountain Shelter after a decent little climb out of Hot Springs.

Part 13

Smokies, Here We Come!

Friday, October 10th
Day 107

Views of the Smokies

I am not sure which was more amazing, Max Patch, or the views of the Smoky Mountains from Max Patch. Max Patch is another "bald" mountain that this area of the country is known for. Acres of beautiful meadows sitting atop large mountains with beautiful views.

From its summit, looking north, we could see the Unaka Mountain Range from which we came. To the east, the Black Mountains, and to the South, the Smokies. They were big, and they were awesome!!!! We are so close to the completion of our journey yet we still have so far to go. I am really looking forward to the Smoky Mountains. It is a place I have always wanted to visit and explore.

Altogether today we hiked 23 miles and climbed some hefty mountains! Very good!

Saturday, October 11th
Day 108

Into the Smokies!
-

Walking into the Smoky Mountains today consisted of a nearly 4000 foot continuous climb up to the summit of Mount Cammerer. The lookout tower at the top is well known for its gorgeous 360 degree views of the surrounding mountains and country side... if only we could see it. Of course, as soon as we began our assent the rains and clouds moved in and shattered any hopes I had of truly enjoying the start of the Smokies. I suppose the rain creates just another way to experience them, but I do wish that I had some views!!

We hiked about 17 miles today through heavy rain and chilly weather. Aeriel and I were fine, but Cameron was NOT having it. He was miserable the whole day. Aeriel and I were in front of him when we made it to Rock Gap Shelter and started to settle in. We built a fire in the shelter's fire place and began to warm up and dry our clothes. As it turns out, most of the shelters in the Smokies come with a built in fire place. How nice.

After about 30 minutes the sun began to set and Cameron still had not shown up – we began to worry. Eventually he did manage to find his way, but he was in the most foul mood and refused to stay at the somewhat crowded shelter with us. He continued down the trail in a huff. The sun was beginning to set and all he had for a light was his small flip phone.

Despite this, he insisted on going an extra 7 miles to the next shelter for reasons unknown to the rational mind. This guy is going to kill himself out here… Its getting dark, he doesn't have a decent light, the weather is awful, and its most likely going to be a cold night. He is literally the poster boy on how to die in the wilderness…Me, I would prefer staying in a nice warm shelter with awesome people. We met two weekend hikers, Ande and Dray, who were a blast to hang out with.

The rain is falling onto the tin roof of the shelter and sounds like the echo of gunshots miles away. The warmth and crackling sounds of the fire rise through the shelter and create the most wonderful homy feel. Altogether, we had a cold and rainy day, yet the grandeur and beauty of the Smokies were not lost on me. They are awesome.

Sunday, October 12th
Day 109

Another Rainy Day

Today was another rainy and overcast day. Despite the weather, the mountains were still incredibly beautiful. We gained another 2000 foot of elevation and then were walking along a high elevation ridgeline all the way to Newfound Gap. The air in the mountains was incredibly fresh and smelt of pine; it reminded me of Christmas. Aeriel and I found Cameron 7 miles up the trail at Tri-Corner Knob shelter. He had survived his night hike in the rain despite not having a proper light; it can't have been much fun for him. He was lucky.

Despite the rain and poor weather, we were able to get a hitch into the wonderful and amazing tourist town of Gatlinburg. The two guys who picked us up were super nice and wanted to know all about our adventure. One of them was a pastor. They drove us all the way to town and were able to drop us off at No-Way Jose – an awesome Mexican restaurant. After days of rain, it was really nice to sit down in a dry and warm place to eat quality food.

Nestled between mountains, Gatlinburg is a very popular spot for hikers, bikers, motorists, and adventurers of every sort. Because of the high number of tourists, countless restaurants, shops, outfitters and hotels have popped up to cater to the high demand. We managed to find a room in a small hotel a few miles up the main strip and settled in for the evening.

Monday, October 13th
Day 110

Gatlinburg
-

Gatlinburg is my kind of town. The dozens of restaurants, shops, and hotels made for a wonderful cocktail of sights and smells. The weather cleared up and the day was sunny and warm – a sharp contrast from the last few days. People were lured out by the hundreds. After so long in the woods and small towns, seeing so many people was somewhat shocking. Quite the sonder experience. I lost count of how many cute girls I saw!

We woke up in the hotel this morning with the intent of relaxing and exploring for most of the day. We watched some weird witch/demon show on the TV (Supernatural?). We got breakfast and walked around town exploring the many shops. Aeriel and I found a trolly and rode it all around Gatlinburg and its surrounding areas. We met a bunch of awesome people on the ride and eventually discovered a Dollar General to resupply at.

After more exploring and hanging out we went to eat at the Mellow Mushroom – a psychedelic type pizza joint. At the bar we ran into a long haired, free-spirited character named Skysurfer. As it turns out he is quite the badass outdoorsy type who hikes, climbs, and adventures in the Smokies. After we ate, he offered to give us a ride back up to Newfound Gap. It's awesome the people you meet!!

As soon as we got back to the trail, clouds moved in once again and we started to hear thunder in the distance... wonderful. Of course, the one day we had great weather we were off trail. I don't get it! Overall, it seems like we have the best luck with the weather, its only when we are in the areas very well-known for their beauty and views that we must contend with rain. I suppose it's a fair trade - you can't win them all.

From Newfound Gap we walked 6 miles to Mt. Collins shelter. On the way, Aeriel and I stopped to wait for Cameron as he had fallen behind again. As has become the norm, we waited, waited, and waited some more for him to show up. After about 30 minutes we were legitimately worried. We had only come a handful of miles and there was no way he should have been *that* far behind. Where could he have gone?!? Once again, Aeriel ran off down the trail to try and find him and I stayed to watch the packs. After just a bit, both Aeriel and Cameron came back. Apparently Cameron, being sad that we "deserted" him again, was just sitting on a rock about a quarter mile back.

What is wrong with this guy?! I am pretty sure that every day he is losing a bit more of his sanity.

We made it to Mt. Collins shelter right as a downpour began. Luckily for us we made it just in time and didn't have to get wet (despite Cameron's best efforts). The shelter was big and, like most shelters in the Smokies, had a built-in fireplace. When we arrived, we found a man and his daughter who had been trying (quite unsuccessfully) to start a fire for the past few hours. Even though everything was soaked, I managed to get enough heat going to dry out some twigs and get a flame. It was wonderful! Everyone was very grateful to me – it felt really good. I like making fires and am actually quite good at it!

Tuesday, October 14th
Day 111

Dry all Day!
-

The rain pounded our shelter all night without reprieve, and when we woke up this morning nothing had changed. It was coming down, and it was coming down hard. We stayed in our sleeping bags with everyone else in the shelter waiting for it to stop, but it never did. As the hours ticked by more and more people decided that they could wait no longer, put on their rain gear, and walked out into the downpour. After a while it was just the three of us left and the rain still showed no signs of slowing. At around noon we decided that we did not want to deal with getting soaked and that we would simply zero in the shelter for the day.

We played lots of canasta and ziggety (among other games). I beat Cameron in Canasta more times than I could count - he was not happy about that! We slept, relaxed, and did quite a bit of nothing all day – it was glorious.

Eventually, a few soaked individuals began to filter into the shelter for the evening. They all seemed incredibly shocked to see three apparent hikers who were dry. We had to explain ourselves to every single new person who showed up. They were all jealous. Despite not moving at all for the day, I am convinced that it was the right move! Who knows how Ol' Cameron would have done in the weather?

Wednesday, October 15th
Day 112

Our Last Day in the Smokies
-

When we woke up this morning, the rain had mostly stopped. Despite this, it was still quite foggy and very humid. However, we couldn't justify staying in the shelter for another day, so we packed up our things and wandered out into the grey misty fog. I was really looking forward to walking up to Clingman's Dome but, of course, all we saw were swirling seas of grey and the occasional pine tree poking out like lonely islands. The alpine regions were still incredibly beautiful, almost beyond description. I can't wait to come back and visit this area again when there is no rain. Mount Washington, Katahdin, and the Smokies are the three main places along the Appalachian Trail that I feel I have not yet experienced to their highest potential. I guess that just means I will need to hike the AT again next year! Oh well!

After Clingmans Dome we began our desent out of the Smokies and eventually ended our day at Derrick Knob Shelter: a total of only 13 miles for the day. If we keep up these very short days, it is possible that we won't finish at all… We were originally planning to go 20 miles and end at Spence Field Shelter but somehow, we convinced ourselves not to.

We shared our shelter with 13 other people, so it was quite crowded. They were all nice though except for a small group who got in late and tried to kick us all out. They had reserved space in the shelter, and despite there still being room for them, they insisted that we all move because:

"WE made reservations! Where are YOUR reservations?".

Well, needless to say, no one who was already there left. Not wanting to share the ample space with so many others, they set up their tent a ways off. Good for them! Everyone else was happy to see them go. As it turns out, no one wants to share a space with such entitled individuals who can't bring themselves to sleep shoulder to shoulder with others. I built another fire and the rest of the evening was quite enjoyable.

I like people, I have decided, socialness is fun.

Thursday, October 16th
Day 113

The Irony
-

Today we hiked 23 miles out of the Smokies. Of course, the twisted minds of the Appalachian Trail gods thought it proper to give us terrible rainy and foggy weather right up until the point where we descended low enough to no longer have views. After that point, the rain and clouds magically disappeared and beautiful sunny skies took their place. The irony was not lost on us.

Our hike today consisted of mostly downhill walking through beautiful forests and along beautiful ridges. We passed "Rocky Top", the summit of which was inspiration for the popular song by the Osborne Brothers by the same name. Of course, we had to sing it out for the world to hear!

We ended the day at Fontana Dam which was awesome. The shelter there, called "The Fontana Hilton" was a bit of a letdown. The view of the lake was wonderful, and the shelter itself was large and had tons of space, but overall, it was nothing special. None of the water fountains there worked. We did, though, have bathrooms with real toilets! We also discovered a bunch of free food and candy. I suppose it was more of a Hilton than we have become accustomed to.

Overall, the experience I had in the Smokies was a good one. Despite the rain and fog we enjoyed ourselves and were still able to appreciate the beauty of the area. I do wish we had some better weather though.

Part 14
The End Days

Friday, October 17th
Day 114

Strange, Unique, and Freakin' Awesome

Today can be summed up by a few words: strange, unique, and freakin' awesome!!!

We walked a total of 15 miles today and ended up at a town called Robbinsville to re-supply. We got a hitch in a from an old guy in a truck. Once we got downtown to the local McDonalds, I got to talking to some nice very country guys doing dip and found out that the local high school was having their homecoming football game tonight. After a few hours at Wendy's and McDonalds (I made some cool north-Carolina hick friends) we decided we would stay in town for the football game.

On the way to the stadium Aeriel needed to pee so we stopped at a gas station where I started talking to the most stereotypical Harley motorcyclists you could imagine about the trip and what we were doing. They were all heavier set and completed the look with leather jackets, long scruffy beards, and dark sunglasses. They seemed in awe of what we had undertaken, and they offered me $50 to "get something good to eat". They insisted that I take nothing less. Sometimes the nicest people in the world are the ones who you least expect.

The football game was tons of fun too. We snuck in because we didn't want to pay the entrance fee and, because the home side was super crowded, decided to go to the away team side. We were promptly chastised and yelled at by an evil cheerleader and an angry mom for commenting on the game (unbiasedly) and trying to explain a rule to her.

On our way out of town we met a pot head who offered to let us camp in his back yard so, of course, we had to take him up on the offer! What an interesting day and interesting town.

Saturday, October 18th
Day 115

The NOC
-

The Nantahala Outdoor Center (referred to simply as "The Noc") is quite the amazing adventure center. Sitting on the Nantahala River it offers adventure seekers an opportunity to raft and kayak the very large and raging river, zipline in the surrounding forests, and participate in numerous outdoor survival and first aid classes! I would love nothing more than to spend a week and a few thousand dollars at this location. If only!

On top of the adventurous opportunities, the NOC also offers a few riverside restaurants and supply options for weary hikers and tourists.

This morning we got up and hitched out of Robbinsville by around 9 o'clock. We took our sweet time, enjoyed numerous breaks, stopped to talk to a bunch of really nice people, and still made it a bit past our 16-mile goal for the day! Awesome!

Of course, Aeriel and Cameron wanted to watch the A&M football game, so we stopped at The River's End restaurant for some Pizza. From the restaurant we had an amazing view of both the game and the river! I was much more interested in the river. Aeriel and Cameron got a beer.

Walking out of the NOC was tedious. Seemingly hundreds of rock stairs wound their way up a few thousand feet to the summit of Wesser Bald. Thankfully, we only had to hike one mile of that climb to get to our campsite for the night: Rufus Morgan Shelter.

Tomorrow morning will probably be difficult.

Sunday, October 19th
Day 116

Monks and Mennonites
-

This morning was difficult indeed. It didn't help matters that we got our now normal late start. Around noon (about 4 miles of walking) we finally made it to the top of Wesser Bald where we discovered an old wooden tower with more amazing 360-degree views. I won't be able to have these kinds of views for much longer. I'm sad.

In many ways, the life of a backpacker is a simple one. The "necessities" of life are all boiled down to their truest form. Food, water, shelter, friendships, and family become easier to understand outside the context of modern life. You carry what you need, and you build stronger relationships with those people you hike with and come across for the first time. I wonder why things get so complicated back home. Perhaps people would get depressed if they realized that they don't actually need half the things they have convinced themselves that they do.

I have gone nearly 120 days now without a cell phone and with very little contact with people from back home. Yet, I am as happy and fulfilled now as I have ever been. I can't imagine what some of my friends back home would do without their technologies.

I don't know. Perhaps everyone should hike the Appalachian Trail. It's eye opening.

We came across a Mennonite couple out walking today as well. They were enjoying the afternoon and were more than happy to stop and chat with us about the trail, and their experiences living in the area. I imagine that they share my thoughts and feelings about simplicity and boiling things down to their purest form. Maybe the Appalachian Trail forces us to do what monks and Mennonites have been doing now for generations.

We walked 16 miles today very slowly. The tough terrain took its toll, but the beauty of the area and the people we met were worth every second of burning thighs.

Monday, October 20th
Day 117

Still Not Ready
-

Yesterday we hiked 16 miles, and today we hiked 16 miles. The difference is that today we also hitched to and from Franklin (a town 10 miles off trail), resupplied at both a Walmart and a Dollar Tree, and found an all-you-can-eat Chinese place! Just goes to show how slowly we took it yesterday.

Our next stop is going to be in Hiawassee, Georgia. At only 50 miles from Springer Mountain, it will be our last and final town stop of the trip. I can't believe it. I'm starting to feel how Gizmo must have felt as he approached Katadin: sad, happy, excited, lost, proud, scared, and a dozen or so other contradictory emotions.

We only have 6 days left on the trail; I can't believe it. Then it's back home and back to school for me. Its going to feel so weird. I feel as if I have gained so many amazing experiences out here. I've met so many wonderful people and have learned so much about myself and my own abilities.

Tuesday, October 21st
Day 118

Already Missing It
-

I am not mentally ready to be done with the trail yet, but I do think the trail is getting closer and closer to being done with us! Winter is coming and it is getting COLD out here! We met this cool thru-hiker named 'Merica and his thermometer says that it is getting down in the mid 30's now! Cold enough for sleet and snow if it decided to rain. Thankfully, it is still sunny.

The leaves have almost all fallen from the trees and the wind, when it picks up, blows through the naked branches with a powerful wooshes. It reminds me of some early childhood memories of running through the Vermont woods at my family's cabin. Its quite a wonderful experience.

I am trying to get ready for not being out here anymore, for not waking up in the quite peacefulness of the woods, for not walking through beautiful countryside and over crazy mountains, for not visiting anymore small towns or meeting any more new people. Its more difficult to make that mental adjustment than you would think it would be.

I feel like I have found a place out here in the woods, a place that I fit into better than at home. I imagine most people on a hike like this are ready to be done once they get to the end. But not me! I'm not sure how many people can truly say that they love being in the wilderness and surrounded by nature, but I certainly do. I will miss it. I already am.

Wednesday, October 22nd
Day 119

The Last State
-

Walking into Hiawassee knowing that it was our last town stop was a surreal experience. 118 days of walking has led us to this moment... our last small Appalachian town.

We got to the road into Hiawassee at around 4:30PM and got a ride in from a gentleman who runs a hostel in the area. Quite the kind and awesome person! We found an all-you-can-eat pizza place as well as a Doller General to resupply at. I would say that our last town stop was a good one!

We hitched out and are now camping near the road. We only have two more nights outside before Our parents drive out to meet us. My dad is planning to finish the last few days with us and we will most likely have a hotel for the last couple days. It really is coming to an end!

We crossed into Georgia today as well! We are officially in the last state! How crazy!

The End

-

When I started my journey, I did not know what I would find. I did not know what to expect. I did not know how it would go. I did not know myself. As it turns out, I knew very little. Now, at the end, I look back and realize that I still know very little. I don't have all the answers to life and happiness. I do, however, know more of myself and know more now than I ever thought I would. In many ways I am the same person as when I started. The trail didn't change that. It did, however, change so much of the way I view myself and the world around me. It has given me so many insights and so many experiences that have shaped me in ways that I am sure that I haven't yet realized. It was nothing like what I expected it would be.

I expected a walk. I expected the rain. I expected the views and the pain. I expected all of this, but those things are not the Appalachian Trail. The Appalachian Trail is not only a journey through a physical space, but a journey through the mind. And it is in the mind that the trail is truly hiked.

In the days that followed Hiawassee we met up with my parents and brother. We enjoyed their company as we finished the precious few miles left to us. Over the heights of Blood, Sassafras, and Hawk Mountains, and through the fall ridden valleys between, we made our way to Springer: the end point of our journey. I I had no choice but to accept the end of this stage of my life. Like the countless rivers and streams we crossed, life must always flow on.

Throughout my travels I cried, I screamed, I was joyous, I was sad. I met hundreds of people and I found myself trusting strangers and putting myself into situations in ways most people would never dream of for fear of something bad happening.

The Appalachian Trail was tremendous. It was a truly maturing experience for me. It was happiness and sorrow. It was living at its most pure and picturesque.

Sure, it was a walk, but in all the ways that matter, it was so much more.

timothy corey

About The Author

Timothy in the Grayson Highlands on the Appalachian Trail in 2014

Timothy was born in Winchester, Massachusetts, in 1998. He lived in New England for 7 years, and in those formative years spent most weekends roaming the Vermont woods at his family's remote cabin with his 4 other siblings. Eight years after completing the Appalachian Trail, Timothy decided to publish his journal.

Timothy has also gone on to complete the Pacific Crest Trail (vlogging along the way) and plans to hike the entire Long Trail with his younger brother in the summer of 2022 – shortly after the publication of this book. He hopes to one-day "triple-crown" by completing the Continental Divide Trail as well, so keep your eyes out for him!!

Timothy currently resides in San Antonio, TX, and has a business degree from the University of Texas at San Antonio. He owns his own marketing company, 7Cs Marketing, and has his own hiking website, timhikes.com. You can watch his hiking videos on his YouTube channel, Tim Hikes.

Did you enjoy this book?

Please leave a review on Amazon by scanning this barcode!

www.ingramcontent.com/pod-product-compliance
Lightning Source LLC
Chambersburg PA
CBHW032150080426
42735CB00008B/657